A Syllabus of Indian Civilization

Prepared as one of the Companions
to Asian Studies

Wm. Theodore de Bary, Editor

A Syllabus of
Indian Civilization

by Leonard A. Gordon
and Barbara Stoler Miller

Columbia University Press

New York & London

1971

FOREWORD

This syllabus is one of a series of aids to the study of Asian civilizations prepared under the auspices of the University Committee on Oriental Studies for use in introductory courses and as a reference for general readers. It is meant to serve as a guide to essential information, bibliography, and questions of general interpretation, not as a cram book or as a substitute for reading and discussion.

Preparation of this syllabus was undertaken at the suggestion of colleagues in Asian studies who felt the need for a syllabus specifically designed for undergraduate education, similar to those which had been prepared for Chinese civilization by J. Mason Gentzler and for Japanese civilization by H. Paul Varley. The present guide has been prepared by two teachers with long experience in the Oriental Studies Program at Columbia and high professional competence in both traditional and modern Indian studies. In a syllabus, however, that experience and competence is shown not in a display of erudition but in the extreme selectivity demanded of its compilers by a work designed to serve general education. Professors Gordon and Miller have met that demand admirably.

Wm. Theodore de Bary

INTRODUCTION

This syllabus is intended for use in introductory courses in Indian civilization. It should serve a variety of functions for teacher and student. We have arranged the forty topics in the sequence which we generally follow in our own course in Indian Civilization and other instructors may wish to use this pattern as well. Within each topic there is a skeleton of concepts and factual information which may be valuable to the student both in the preliminary grasping of a difficult subject and in reviewing an area after he has participated in classes and is reflecting upon what he has learned. The annotated reading assignments and suggestions and the discussion questions are meant to send the student deeper into his study of Indian civilization.

Arrangement of topics. The material is arranged to stress the characteristic features of Indian civilization within an historical framework. We have followed the broad line of historical development in India and within this context we have tried to suggest the interplay of historical forces and specific cultural, religious, literary, political, and economic developments. We have been influenced in our approach by historically-minded anthropologists and culturally-minded historians, whose treatment of things Indian has seemed most fruitful to us. We have tried to consider ideas within their relevant historical situations in order to illuminate them, as well as considering the general view of political and cultural history. But like any syllabus or series of outlines, the elements in our syllabus are only a beginning to which student and teacher add flesh and muscle, elaborated content, further detail, and richness.

In the traditional section, major religious, social, and cultural developments which overlap defined chronological periods are necessarily introduced as separate topics. In the modern section, the movement of topics is from a concentration on imperialism and British in India to a concentration on nationalism and the Indians.

Readings. We have grouped readings into three categories: assigned, optional, and additional readings. The reading assignments are designed for a shorter course with a minimum of essential material. The optional assignments include readily available books and articles which offer more detail and greater scope than the assigned readings. The additional readings are meant to send the student on to more advanced study of particular topics. We further suggest that students make use of some of the valuable bibliographic aids for South Asian studies, including the annual bibliographic issue of the *Journal of Asian Studies;* J. Michael Mahar, *India, A Critical Bibliography* (Tucson: University of Arizona Press, 1964); Maureen L.P. Patterson and Ronald B. Inden, *South Asia: An Introductory Bibliography* (Chicago: University of Chicago Press, 1962; new edition in preparation); and Margaret H. Case, *South Asian History 1750–1950, A Guide to Periodicals, Dissertations, and Newspapers* (Princeton: Princeton University Press, 1968). Also of value is Robert I. Crane's bibliographic essay, "The History of India: Its Study and Interpretation," Publication Number 17, Service Center for Teachers of History, Washington, D.C., 1958.

Maps. We have added a series of maps which illustrate significant geographical and historical features of the South Asian subcontinent. Of great value in this connection is C. Collin Davies, *A Historical Atlas of the Indian Peninsula* (London: Oxford University Press, 1959, second edition).

We would like to thank Philip B. Calkins of the University of Chicago, who assisted us greatly in the preparation of the topics covering Muslim expansion and rule in India. We also benefited from the critical comments of Ainslie T. Embree, Duke University, Wm. Theodore de Bary and John Meskill, Columbia University, and Ronald B. Inden, University of Chicago. Of course, we take responsibility for the arrangement for topics, choice of details, and other materials contained in this syllabus.

Columbia University   Barbara Stoler Miller
March, 1971   Leonard A. Gordon

CONTENTS

Traditional India

BOOKS FOR ASSIGNED READINGS

General Readings on Traditional India

Cohn, Bernard S. *India: The Social Anthropology of a Civilization.* Englewood Cliffs, New Jersey: Prentice-Hall, 1971. An attempt by a historian-anthropologist to examine India as a civilization, a social system, a nation existing in time as well as in space. Contemporary structural-functional techniques of analysis are applied to present an integrated study of "primitive" and "modern" societies.

Davies, C. Collin. *An Historical Atlas of the Indian Peninsula.* London: Oxford University Press paperback, 1957. Maps and accompanying text concentrate on the geography of political entities from the sixth century B.C. to modern times; also includes maps of general geographic features.

de Bary, Wm. Theodore (ed.). *Sources of Indian Tradition.* New York: Columbia University Press, 1958. Paperback, (in two volumes), 1964. Source readings illustrating major aspects of Indian intellectual and religious thought, accompanied by excellent essays and introductions. Page references are for the hardcover edition and volume I of the paperback.

Kosambi, D.D. *Ancient India: A History of Its Culture and Civilization.* New York: Pantheon, 1965. Paperback, 1970. A history of ancient India which draws on archaeological, anthropological, and historical evidence to support a Marxist view of historical development. Often overly speculative, but rich in stimulating ideas and questions.

Spear, Percival. *A History of India.* Volume 2. Baltimore: Penguin, Pelican paperback, 1965. This survey of the period after 1500 is the companion to Thapar's volume; begins with a good account of the Mughals, providing a transition from traditional to modern India.

Thapar, Romila. *A History of India*. Volume 1. Baltimore: Penguin, Pelican paperback, 1966. A survey of events and culture from the coming of the Indo-Aryans until the arrival of the Europeans in the sixteenth century. Social and economic rather than religious institutions are stressed as the key to political and cultural developments. Extensive reference is made to studies of social organization and to archaeological evidence.

Other Recommended General Readings

Basham, A.L. *The Wonder That Was India*. New York: Macmillan, 1954. Grove Press paperback, 1959. A survey of various aspects of classical Indian culture, including politics, social structure, religion, arts, and literature. An excellent introduction; well illustrated.

Majumdar, Ramesh C. (general ed.). *The History and Culture of the Indian People*. Volumes I–VI. Bombay: Bharatiya Vidya Bhavan, 1951–1960. A detailed account of the political, socioeconomic, and cultural history of India written by a team of about sixty India scholars. Volumes I–VI deal with the major periods of ancient, classical, and medieval Indian history. To be consulted for depth reading on aspects of any period.

Majumdar, R.C., H.C. Raychaudhuri, and Kalikinkar Datta. *An Advanced History of India*. London: Macmillan, 1960. Paperback, 1969. General survey, covering cultural as well as political developments; same nationalist bias which characterizes the multivolume *History and Culture of the Indian People*.

Smith, Vincent A. *The Oxford History of India*. Third edition, edited by Percival Spear. Oxford: Clarendon Press, 1961. Paperback, 1967. A detailed survey, first published in 1919, somewhat pro-British in tone. Recent revisions have failed to bring its point of view up to date; still a sound single-volume reference work.

4

I. GEOGRAPHY OF THE SUBCONTINENT

A. Natural boundaries: Himalayas, Punjab hills and desert, jungle-covered mountains of Assam, Arabian Sea, Bay of Bengal
B. Typographic variety throughout subcontinent
    1. Mountain and hill areas: Himalayan foothills; Vindhya range, Satpura and Mahadeo-Maikala hill systems; Eastern and Western Ghats; Nilgiri and Palni hills
    2. Deserts of Punjab, Rajasthan, Central India
    3. Deccan Plateau
    4. Great Northern or Indo-Gangetic Plain
        a. Indus river system
        b. Alluvial Ganges Valley
    5. Wet lowlands of Lower Ganges, Bengal; Orissa-Andhra, Madras, Malabar, and Konkan coasts
C. Climatic variety according with topographic variety; characteristic climatic rigors
    1. Wet agriculture dependent on annual southwest monsoon (see Map 1)
        a. Movement of rain-bearing air during summer season ("monsoon" derived from Arabic word for season)
        b. Timing and adequate rainfall determine success of monsoon; 50 percent deficit means famine, overabundance means flooding
    2. Arid and semi-arid expanses, dependent on irrigation
D. Geography and crops
    1. Chief food crops: rice, wheat; lesser crops: millet, maize, pulses, spices, sugarcane; commercial crops: cotton, jute, tobacco, tea
    2. Monsoon areas produce rice
    3. Semi-arid areas produce wheat
    4. Irrigation: river-fed systems, wells, artificial storage tanks
    5. Methods of cultivation: seasonal variation, labor, implements
E. Geography and historical developments

1. Mountain systems as barriers
   a. Himalayas account for weakness of contact with China
   b. Interior systems: obstacles to invaders (relative isolation of South India); refuges
   c. Invaders from Central Asian grasslands funnel into Northwest; vulnerability of the Northwest and Ganges Plain
2. Sea travel: trade routes
   a. Contacts with Near East and West
   b. Relations with Southeast Asia
3. Population migrations, ethnic mixtures
4. Urbanization
5. Linguistic diversities
   a. Major language families
      1) Indo-Aryan
      2) Dravidian
      3) Munda
      4) Tibeto-Burman
   b. Dialect variants

Reading Assignment

Cohn, *India: Social Anthropology,* 1–51
Davies, *Historical Atlas,* 5, 76–89

Optional Assignment

Rawson, R.R. *Monsoon Lands of Asia.* Chicago: Aldine paperback, 1963. A nontechnical account of the geography of monsoon-dependent areas, followed by examination of distinctive aspects of the main political units, including India. A good introduction to this dominating feature of Indian civilization.

Additional Readings

Davis, Kingsley. *The Population of India and Pakistan.* Princeton: Princeton University Press, 1951. Somewhat outdated, but still the best demographic study of South Asia, based on census information from 1872–1941; discusses historical, geographic, and social factors relevant to population growth and change.
Ginsburg, Norton (ed.). *The Pattern of Asia.* Englewood Cliffs, New Jersey: Prentice-Hall, 1958. Pp. 458–697 contain a good description of the physical, economic, and political geography of South Asia.
Spate, O.H.K., and A.T.A. Learmonth. *India and Pakistan: A General and Regional Geography.* Revised edition. London: Methuen,

1967. The standard work on the geography of the Indian subcontinent, dealing with land, people, and economy in detail. Maps, tables.

Discussion Topics and Questions

1. What are the general effects of geography on cultural patterns and the development of civilizations?
2. What are the significant linguistic, cultural, and political regions of the Indian subcontinent? How do they change in time? And what importance does this have for the development of Indian civilization?

II. INDIAN CIVILIZATION: UNITY AND DIVERSITY

A. Records of premodern Indian civilization
  1. Dearth of written records until the sixteenth century
    a. Scanty historical materials prior to 300 B.C.
      1) Archaeological evidence; undeciphered Harappan seals
      2) Literature of myth and legend: Vedic hymns, Epic poems, Buddhist texts
      3) Foreign sources: Mesopotamian, Greek
      4) Anthropological studies of different cultural patterns (e.g. tribal, village; Hindu, non-Hindu); describe and suggest variety of possible ways of life on subcontinent, past and present
    b. Fuller historical records from 300 B.C. to sixteenth century A.D.
      1) Royal inscriptions, land-grant plates, coin issues, genealogies
      2) Records of foreign travelers: Greek writers, Chinese Buddhist pilgrims
      3) Court epics
      4) Muslim chronicles
  2. Mughal court histories
  3. Religious texts; continuity of religious traditions over 4,000 years
    a. Priestly class (Brahman) bias in ancient religious and literary texts; tendency of Brahman specialists to rewrite legends, reinterpret observances, synthesize sectarian differences; the status position of Sanskrit

7

  b. Other textual traditions: Jain, Buddhist

  c. Sectarian, local, unorthodox religious literature

B. A general view of civilization in India

  1. Peaks in the flow of history: e.g., Indus Valley civilization, Mauryan empire, Muslim civilization; characterized by centralized political organization, cultural efflorescence

  2. Cultural continuities (processes and ideals): a characteristically "Indian" way of life, extensive in time and space

    a. Specific elements as sources of generalizations: a village, an individual case history, a caste, a festival, a particular text, a dynasty, an historic event

    b. Diverse cultural levels of sources

      1) Civilized and primitive

      2) City, village, tribe

      3) Universal and local, "great" and "little" traditions

    c. Continual processes of cultural transmission: interacting traditions; systems of communication and structural integration

      1) Adoption of standardized behavior by isolated groups

      2) Influence of diverse cultures on the standard

Reading Assignments

Cohn, *India: Social Anthropology*, 1–7, 51–97 (an overview)
Kosambi, *Ancient India*, 8–25
Thapar, *History of India*, 15–23

Optional Assignments

Redfield, Robert. "Civilizations as Things Thought About," in Margaret Redfield (ed.), *Human Nature and the Study of Society, The Papers of Robert Redfield.* Volume I, 364–75. Chicago: University of Chicago Press, 1962.

Wolf, Eric. *Peasants.* Foundations of Modern Anthropology Series. Englewood Cliffs, New Jersey: Prentice-Hall, 1966. A lucid statement of the role of peasants in the evolution of human society; relevant to the development of Indian civilization, past and present.

Additional Readings

Brown, W. Norman. *Man in the Universe: Some Continuities in Indian Thought.* Berkeley: University of California Press, 1966. Paperback, 1970. A series of lectures analyzing the vitalizing elements which have given Hindu culture its uniqueness and continuity.

Brown, W. Norman. "Mythology of India," in S.N. Kramer (ed.), *Mythologies of the Ancient World*. Garden City, New York: Doubleday, Anchor paperback, 1961, 275–330. Brief illuminating statements of various types of mythology which have served as "symbolizing ideas" in the development of Indian religious thought.

Majumdar, Ramesh C. (ed.). Introduction. *The History and Culture of the Indian People*. Volume I, *The Vedic Age*, book I, 31–66. Bombay: Bharatiya Vidya Bhavan, 1951. Discussion of the nature, scope, method, and sources of Indian history by the editor of the "first history of India, written exclusively by her own people."

Singer, Milton (ed.). *Traditional India: Structure and Change*. Philadelphia: American Folklore Society, 1959. A collection of excellent essays on characteristic aspects of Indian tradition.

Vansina, Jan. *Oral Tradition: A Study in Historical Methodology*. Translated from the French by H.M. Wright. Chicago: Aldine, 1965. Explores the possibility of reconstructing the history of nonliterate peoples from their oral traditions.

Discussion Topics and Questions

1. Who in India is "civilized"? Consider the various approaches to the study of civilization in formulating your criteria. Evaluate criteria such as class differentiation and specialization, urbanization, social heterogeneity, systematic record-keeping. Examine, with special reference to India, Eric Wolf's statement that the development of civilization is "the development of a complex social order based on a division between rulers and food-producing cultivators." (*Peasants*, p. 4)

2. Discuss the nature of "urban revolution" in the history of Indian civilization—compare with other ancient and modern urban revolutions.

3. How static is "tradition"? What institutions and groups in Indian society are the bearers of tradition? What is the nature of their status positions?

4. What significance does the role of the Brahman priesthood have for the development of characteristic Indian political and social institutions (cf. the role of the bureaucracy in Chinese civilization)? What kinds of problems are inherent in the Indian pattern of relations between religious authority and secular administration?

9

5. What forces for unity and diversity are significant in different regions and at various stages in Indian history?

III. PREHISTORY AND HARAPPAN CIVILIZATION

A. Prehistoric periods of various regions and societies differ: no single prehistoric chronology for subcontinent
  1. Paleolithic food-gatherers
  2. Microlithic transitional cultures: some pottery, evidence of cultivated plants
  3. Neolithic cultures: settled life, animal husbandry, some form of cultivation, stone implements, pottery
    a. Precursors to Harappan civilization: Iranian plateau, cultures of Baluchistan hills (fourth to third millenium B.C.)
    b. Neolithic-Chalcolithic cultures beyond the Indus system, contemporaneous with and succeeding Harappan civilization
    c. Isolated hill and forest tribal societies: remnants in modern times
B. Harappan civilization: enigmatic protohistory (ca. 3000–1500 B.C.)
  1. Origins: who were the Harappans?
    a. Ambiguous physical anthropological evidence; dispute as to connection with Australoid and/or Dravidian peoples of later Indian culture.
    b. Recent work on undeciphered Harappan inscriptions suggests script represents proto-Dravidian: were Harappans Dravidians?
  2. Spatial and temporal limits of Harappan civilization
    a. Indus rivers, flowing in alluvial desert, lured mountain people; confines of valley conducive to the rise of civilization
    b. Recent excavations extend Indus axis: Arabian Sea north to Simla hills; east to Ganges-Jamna Plain; south to Gulf of Cambay; network of cities
    c. Dating
      1) Mesopotamian contacts (ca. 2300–1700 B.C.)
      2) Radiocarbon dates, ambiguous
      3) 1965 excavations at Mohenjo-Daro: lowest strata antedate Mesopotamian contacts

3. Economic support of the civilization
    a. Agricultural society
        1) Produce: wheat; also barley, peas, melon, sesame, cotton
        2) Flood irrigation; rich silt, no deep plowing needed; fire and stone tools suffice
        3) Domestic animals: humped and humpless cattle, buffalo, goats, sheep, pigs, dogs
    b. Extensive trade
        1) Overland caravan, river, and sea routes (Lothal, port)
        2) Known imports: gold, copper, lapis lazuli from Afghanistan, Iran, South India; ornaments of faience, stone, gold show links with civilizations of the West
        3) External evidence: Indus seals found in Mesopotamian sites
4. Material evidence suggests complex patterns of life
    a. Cities built on elaborate principles of planning, reflective of centralized authority, social stratification, craft specialization; probably also of strong organized religion
        1) Principal cities, Mohenjo-Daro and Harappa
        2) "Citadel" mound dominating cities (cf. Mesopotamian ziggurat); Mohenjo-Daro tank (for ritual bathing?); granary, planned streets, drains, bathrooms, fine brickwork
    b. Written records: undeciphered inscriptions on distinctive steatite intaglio seals, probably used in controlling trade and administration
        1) Inscriptions in pictographic script; probably represent proper names of gods, high officials, institutions, individuals
        2) Accompanying iconographic devices include animals (natural and composite), anthropomorphic figures (e.g. "proto-Shiva"?), abstract patterns
    c. Sculpture and seals show motifs associated with agricultural cults, e.g. terracotta animals, mother-goddess (?) figurines, phallic stones
    d. Individual sculpture works of high artistic quality, e.g. modeled stone torsos, "priest-king" bust, bronze "dancing girl" figurine
    e. Mass-produced pottery: wheel-turned, pinkish or buff ware with red slip, abstract and pictorial motifs, a few inscriptions

11

f. Variety of tools: stone and copper-bronze knives, swords, spears, arrowheads, axes, fishhooks
C. Fragmentation of Harappan civilization: archaeological evidence suggests natural and human pressures
   1. Geographical changes: coastal uplift, abnormal flooding
     a. Souring and erosion of the land
     b. Economic decline reflected in lowered civic standards and cultural collapse
   2. Weakened cities overcome by waves of Aryan invaders from northwest
     a. Achaeological evidence for Indo-Aryans in Punjab: graves, pottery, copperhoards
     b. *Ṛg Veda* hymns: references to Punjab rivers, to battles with dark-skinned, snub-nosed people who are phallus worshippers, cattle keepers, city dwellers; also references to "ruined sites"; does reference to Hariyupiya equal Harappa?

Reading Assignments

Kosambi, *Ancient India*, 26–71
Thapar, *History of India*, 23–27

Optional Assignment

Wheeler, Mortimer. *Civilizations of the Indus Valley and Beyond.* New York: McGraw Hill paperback, 1966. A survey of South Asian prehistory to the third century B.C., including appraisal of unsolved problems and recent excavations. Nontechnical and profusely illustrated. Pp. 1–92 deal with Harappan civilization.

Additional Readings

Allchin, Bridget and Raymond. *The Birth of Indian Civilization.* Baltimore: Penguin Books, Pelican paperback, 1968. A detailed introduction to Indian prehistory and protohistory, based on recent excavations and radiocarbon datings. Somewhat technical, well illustrated. Excellent bibliography. Updates Stuart Piggott's *Prehistoric India* (London, 1950. Penguin reprint, 1961).
Childe, V. Gordon. *New Light on the Most Ancient East.* New York: Praeger, 1954. Evergreen Press paperback, 1962. Discussion of the Indus Valley civilization in relation to Egypt and Mesopotamia.
Parpola, Asko, with Seppo Koskenniemi, Simo Parpola, and Pentti Aalto. *Decipherment of the Proto-Dravidian Inscriptions of the*

Indus Civilization: A First Announcement. Copenhagen: The Scandinavian Institute of Asian Studies, 1969. Reviewed and criticized by Thomas R. Trautman in the *Journal of Asian Studies,* XXIX, no. 3 (1970), 714–16; also by John Chadwick and Gerard Clauson, "The Indus Script Deciphered?" *Antiquity,* XLIII, no. 171 (September, 1969), 200–207.

Discussion Topics and Questions

1. Do pre-Harappan cultures in the northwest and the Indus Valley provide essential elements for the evolution of Harappan civilization? Why was there urbanization at Indus sites?
2. Examine Harappan city plans and structures; compare with those of contemporaneous Mesopotamian cities.
3. Analyze formal and functional aspects of Harappan artifacts. What do they suggest about the quality of Indus city life?
4. Study visually and analyze the content of the Harappan seals. Note distinctive motifs with an eye for their recurrence in later Indian culture.

IV. THE ARYAN INVADERS
(ca. 1800–1000 B.C.)

A. Nomadic tribes bound by closely related dialects of parent language
   1. Designated themselves Aryan, term denoting their racial superiority ("noble," "respectable") vs. pre-existing peoples of India
   2. Indo-European origins: linguistic and limited archaeological evidence
      a. Proto-Indo-European reconstructed from grammar and vocabulary of cognate languages, e.g., Celtic, Slavic, Indic, Greek
      b. Linguistic and archaeological evidence points to homeland in south Russian-Ukrainian steppes
      c. Dispersal
         1) Domestication of horse, use of light war chariot (ca. 2000 B.C.)
         2) Inscriptional evidence of Indo-European names, gods, terms in Asia Minor by ca. 1800 B.C.

      3) Hittite-Mitanni treaty of ca. 1380 B.C. mentions Vedic gods; Boghaz Keui tablets on horse training use Sanskrit terms

      4) Archaeological evidence of post-Harappan "Jhukar" culture, Harappa Cemetery H (ca. 1750–1400 B.C.); copper-bronze implements, pottery (Iranian affinities); hypothesis of cultural fusion of Harappan and foreign elements

B. Vedic literature represents earliest records of Aryan culture in India, Aryan viewpoint of history

  1. Sacred oral tradition, maintained for about thirty centuries (ca. 1400 B.C.–A.D. 1400)

  2. Transmitted by memory from Brahman teacher to pupil; Brahman monopoly

  3. Two main classes

    a. Verse collections (ca. 1400–1000 B.C.): *Ṛg Veda, Yajur Veda, Sāma Veda;* later *Atharva Veda*

    b. Expository prose (ca. 1000–300 B.C.): Brahmanas, Aranyakas, Upanishads

  4. *Ṛg Veda,* basic anthology of hymns, mainly composed while Aryans in northwest: epic chants, hymns of praise, prayers to gods, magic spells; elaborate language and metrical structure

    a. Hymns descriptive of pastoral culture, compatible with archaeological evidence

      1) Material characteristics: wagons, light chariots; domesticated horses, sheep, goats, cattle (wealth measured in cattle); cultivated barley and wheat; copper-bronze tools and weapons

      2) Social organization and class specialization: warriors (hereditary lineage of chiefs); priests; householders; servants and laborers

      3) Geography centered in Punjab ("land of the five waters")

    b. Hymns composed to accompany fire cult: domestic hearth rites, seasonal and special public sacrifices (yajna); priests officiate on behalf of warriors

      1) Materialistic orientation: wealth, health, sons, victory in war

      2) Hymns composed by inspired poet-priests to invoke gods; prayer considered to have magic potency (brahman)

      3) Esoteric ritual: preparation of sacred ground, fire, intoxicating plant juice (soma), animal sacrifice

4) Sympathetic magic: correct performance of ritual co-
erces gods and controls universe
c. Rich mythology: natural, ritual, and historical aspects of
experience apotheosized, generally Indo-European gods;
tendency towards "henotheism"
1) Indra: thunder, monsoon god, soma-drinker, barbarian
battle-leader, cattle-raider who destroys enemies' strong-
holds, order-bringer; Aryan (Vritra: drought, darkness,
confusion, evil hoarder, Indra's archenemy; non-Aryan)
2) Agni: fire, divine priest, intermediary between men and
gods, consumer of the enemy
3) Varuna: sky, righteous sovereign of gods and men, up-
holder of moral and cosmic order (vrata, "personal
vow"; rita, "cosmic order")
d. Speculative thought: later books of *Ṛg Veda; Atharva
Veda*
1) Search for occult correspondences: men–gods; perform-
ers of sacrifice–creators of universe; microcosm–macro-
cosm; to ensure rewards of sacrifice and order in cosmic
and mundane realms
2) To know something is to control it: impetus to knowledge
3) Scepticism about efficacy of gods, especially Indra

Reading Assignments

Kosambi, *Ancient India,* 72–81
Thapar, *History of India,* 28–49
Sources of Indian Tradition, 1–20; paperback, 1–19

Optional Assignment

Zaehner, R.C. (ed. and tr.). *Hindu Scriptures.* New York: Dutton
Everyman's Library, 1966. New translations of selected Vedic
hymns, Upanishads, and the *Bhagavad Gītā;* the best single volume of these brahmanical Hindu scriptures. Pp. 3–30 include
hymns from the *Ṛg Veda* and the *Atharva Veda.*

Additional Readings

Allchin, Bridget and Raymond. *The Birth of Indian Civilization.*
Pp. 144–56. See III above. This section discusses archaeological
evidence relating to the Aryan invasions.
Bloomfield, Maurice (tr.). *Hymns of the Atharva Veda.* Sacred Books
of the East, volume 42. Oxford, Clarendon Press, 1897. To be re-

issued in paperback by Dover. A scholarly translation of selections from the latest collection of Vedic hymns, notable for charms. See also the translator's classic monograph, *The Atharva Veda*. Strassburg: Trubner, 1899.

Burrow, Thomas. *The Sanskrit Language*. London: Faber and Faber, 1955. An account of the history, structure, and characteristic achievement of Vedic and post-Vedic Sanskrit, with emphasis on its relations to other Indo-European languages.

Griffith, Ralph T.H. *The Hymns of the Ṛgveda: Translated with a Popular Commentary*. Two volumes. Third edition. Banaras: E.J. Lazarus, 1920–1926. Reprint, Banaras: Chowkhamba Sanskrit Studies, volume XXXV, 1963. The only complete translation of the *Ṛg Veda* in English; archaic and often inaccurate.

Keith, Arthur B. *The Religion and Philosophy of the Vedas and Upaniṣads*. Harvard Oriental Series, volumes 31 and 32. Cambridge: Harvard University Press, 1925. A detailed scholarly survey of Vedic literature; comparisons with other Indo-European and non-Vedic Indian cultures are notable.

Macdonell, Arthur A. *A History of Sanskrit Literature*. New York: Appleton, 1900. Reprint, Delhi: Munshi Ram Manohar Lal, 1961, 1–172. Macdonell's treatment of the historical development and content of Vedic literature is sympathetic and well illustrated with his own translations.

Majumdar, Ramesh C. (ed.). *The History and Culture of the Indian People*. Volume I, *The Vedic Age*, books III–VII. Bombay: Bharatiya Vidya Bhavan, 1951. A detailed survey of the period to 600 B.C. by various Indian scholars, including accounts of literary, political, religious, and socioeconomic conditions. Some interpretations of Aryan culture are controversial.

Müller, F.M. and H. Oldenberg (tr.). *Vedic Hymns*. Sacred Books of the East, volumes 32 and 36. Oxford: Clarendon Press, 1891–1897. To be reprinted in paperback by Dover. A scholarly translation of major portions of the *Ṛg Veda*, the most ancient of the collections of Vedic hymns.

Renou, Louis. *Religions of Ancient India*. London: Athlone Press, 1953. Schocken paperback, 1968. The chapters on Vedism (1–45) are an authoritative survey of the subject and its challenges to scholarship.

Smith, H. Daniel (ed.). *Selections from Vedic Hymns*. Berkeley: McCutcheon paperback, 1968. About 80 Vedic hymns in translation; a thematic introduction to the literature.

Discussion Topics and Questions

1. Contrast the culture of the pastoral Aryans with that of the agricultural, city-dwelling Harappans. Keep the diversity of evidence in mind.
2. Compare elements of the Vedic fire cult with known Harappan cult elements.
3. The meaning, significance, and history of the term "Aryan."
4. The relation between Indic and other Indo-European mythologies and religions (e.g., see Fustel de Coulanges, *The Ancient City,* which describes the religious foundations of civic life in Greece and Rome; many Indian parallels).
5. The position of warrior and priest in Vedic society as reflected in the hymns. What tools of power did the priest wield?
6. The nature of oral literary tradition; institutions providing for accurate oral transmission of Vedic literature.
7. Biases inherent in reading the *Ṛg Veda* as an account of historic events.
8. The place of magic in Vedic religion; the relation between magic and speculative thought.

V. ARYAN EXPANSION AND CIVILIZATION
(ca. 1000–300 B.C.)

A. Settlement of the Ganges-Jamna Basin: fertile riverside clearings in jungle, shift to sedentary life
  1. Archaeological evidence of eastward movement: urban sites, e.g., Hastinapur levels; shift to sedentary style of life
    a. Ca. 800–500 B.C.: Painted Grey Ware, copper, iron, mud brick walls
    b. Ca. 500–200 B.C.: Northern Black Polished Ware, iron, baked brick buildings, city plan, coinage
  2. Literary evidence of civic life: *Śatapatha Brāhmaṇa;* epics, e.g., Hastinapur as capital of Kaurava kings; breakup of old tribal groups; extensive agriculture
B. Peninsula colonization: Aryan minority
  1. Archaeological evidence: iron, Black-and-Red Ware/Northern-Black-Polished Ware sequences; burial complexes, "megaliths"

2. *Rāmāyaṇa* as allegory of Aryan attempt to conquer South? (cf. Rama-Ravana duel, Vedic Indra-Vritra duel)

C. Civilization of Aryan culture
1. Monarchies deriving revenue from agriculture
   a. Organization for clearance of rain forest land, river trade
   b. King as protector of people, maintainer of class laws
   c. Tax collection: hierarchy of officers, village as basic unit of administration
2. Development of law and legal institutions; religious duty (dharma): sanctification of customary conduct, morality, and law
3. Class distinctions; exclusivism of "twice-born"
4. Systematization of education: limited to upper classes, Brahmanic dominance
   a. Teacher (guru) to student (brahmachari), transmission of knowledge
   b. Stress on elaborate rituals and cultivation of memory
5. Codification of Sanskrit by grammarian Panini (ca. 500 B.C.): official, literary language of educated; status language
6. Challenges to Vedic social, religious orthodoxy: asceticism vs. society; wisdom and meditation vs. sacrificial ritual
7. Philosophical speculation: the Upanishads (secret communications); called Vedanta (the end of the Veda)
   a. Dialogues search for mystery of cosmos, man's relation to it; not systematic philosophy
   b. Pantheistic mysticism: reality is universal, the individual (atman) is the universe (brahman)
   c. Knowledge brings immortality, limitless mystical power
8. Composition of epic poetry: professional minstrels appeal to popular taste
   a. *Mahābhārata*
      1) Epic kernel, war between the Kauravas and Pandavas
      2) Encyclopedia of moral teaching
   b. *Rāmāyaṇa*
      1) Homogeneous work of art, ornate poetry (kavya)
      2) Idealized characters: hero-prince Rama, faithful wife Sita, demon Ravana

Reading Assignments

Kosambi, *Ancient India*, 81–95
Sources of Indian Tradition, 20–36; paperback, 19–34

Optional Assignments

Narayan, R.K. *Gods, Demons, and Others*. New York: Viking paperback, 1964. Tales from the ancient epics retold by one of India's leading English novelists. A lively introduction to the storehouse of epic legends and beliefs.

Wheeler, Mortimer. *Civilizations of the Indus Valley and Beyond*. See III above; 93–103 deal with post-Indus civilization evidence.

Zaehner, R.C. (ed. and tr.). *Hindu Scriptures*. See IV above; 33–245 include selections from the major Upanishads.

Additional Readings

Allchin, Bridget and Raymond. *The Birth of Indian Civilization*. Pp. 207–32. See III above. Archaeological evidence of the Iron Age and beginnings of history.

Edgerton, Franklin. *The Beginnings of Indian Philosophy*. Cambridge: Harvard University Press, 1965. Selected Vedic texts translated with introduction and notes, to show the early development of Hindu philosophy.

Hume, Robert E. *The Thirteen Principal Upanishads*. Second edition. London: Oxford University Press, 1931. Best English translation of the major Upanishads.

Keith, Arthur B. *The Religion and Philosophy of the Vedas and Upaniṣads*. See IV above. Part V deals with Vedic philosophy.

Narasimhan, C.V. *The Mahābhārata*. New York: Columbia University Press, 1964. A prose translation of the main epic narrative.

Shastri, Hari Prasad. *The Ramayana of Valmiki*. Three volumes. London: Shanti Sadan, 1952–1959. Complete prose translation, somewhat stiff, but readable.

For further bibliography and topics on the Vedas, Upanishads, and Epics see *A Guide to Oriental Classics*, edited by Wm. T. de Bary and Ainslie Embree. New York: Columbia University Press, 1964, 43–59.

Discussion Topics and Questions

1. Elements in the process by which the barbarian Aryans were "civilized"; new ideals and institutions, e.g., the changing roles of the culture hero, the priest.
2. The implications of asceticism as a cultural ideal.
3. The pedagogic techniques of the Upanishadic sages; the pursuit and rewards of mystical knowledge.

4. The meaning and appeal of *Mahābhārata* motifs, allegories, characters, ethics.
5. The *Rāmāyaṇa* as court epic and mythology; the interplay of human and supernatural levels; the nature of destiny, duty, tragedy, love.

VI. THE HETERODOXIES: JAINISM AND BUDDHISM

A. Origins: Eastern Ganges Basin, Himalayan foothills (seventh to fifth centuries B.C.)
　1. Political setting, contrast between political and social organization of Upper Ganges and that of Middle Ganges
　　a. Regional kingdoms: Avanti, Vatsa, Kosala, Magadha; Magadhan ascendency: Kings Bimbasara, Ajatashatru
　　b. Territories ruled by acephalous lineages: governed by popuplar assembly and elders
　　　1) Vaggian Confederacy of several clans, including Licchavis, Jnatrikas
　　　2) Independent clans, e.g. Shakyas, Mauryas
　　c. Expansion of towns, based on rich rice culture of Eastern Ganges: landed aristocracy, rich merchants, free peasant populations; advanced material culture, commerce, trade (Persian, South Indian contacts)
　2. Intellectual developments
　　a. Upanishadic speculations based on Vedas; adopted by orthodox Brahmans as Vedic ancillaries
　　b. Various atheistic sects rejecting Vedas, Vedic ritual; Buddhism and Jainism most enduring
B. Jainism: ancient teachings given shape by Mahavira (great hero), ca. 540–468 B.C., called Jina (conqueror) referring to his victory over karma, samsara
　1. Gods irrelevant to salvation; eternal cosmic laws, waves of progress and decline that govern universe
　2. Everything in universe (rocks, plants) has degree of soul or life (jiva); soul-matter dualism
　3. Purification through ahimsa; nonviolence as enlightened self-interest: all action injures, binds actor; soul's freedom from matter depends on non-action
　4. Knowledge inadequate for salvation: all knowledge is rela-

20

tive; parable of six blind men describing elephant in terms of parts touched

C. Buddhism: teachings of Siddhartha Gautama, the Buddha (enlightened one) ca. 563–483 B.C.; first recorded in Pali Discourses (suttas)
  1. Four sights, insights: old man, sick man, corpse (transiency, life is suffering); monk (seeking salvation in renunciation)
  2. Enlightenment through meditation
  3. Defeat of Mara (death, demonic lord of instinctual life)
  4. Buddha's Way (dharma; Pali, dhamma)
    a. Psychological diagnosis and prescription
    b. First sermon at Deer Park; nucleus of teaching in Four Noble Truths ("Aryan truths" example of Buddha's ironical use of brahmanic words)
      1) Life is suffering
      2) Craving for permanence is cause
      3) Cessation of cause
      4) By means of eightfold path—the "middle way," practical method between egotistic extremes of indulgence, asceticism
  5. Causal analyses of problems: dependent origination, wheel of rebirth
  6. Salvation in nirvana: extinction of craving; release from endless chain of samsara

D. Common characteristics shared by Jainism and Buddhism
  1. Legendary lives of founders similar; examples for followers
    a. After many previous existences as many kinds of beings, miraculous conception, celebrated birth in royal families (Buddha, Shakya son of warrior chief; Mahavira, Jnatrika chief's son)
    b. Renunciation of worldly life to seek salvation, wandering and asceticism
    c. Enlightenment, teaching, death
  2. Egalitarianism
    a. Birth no criterion of worth; opposed to Brahman exclusiveness, expensive ritual, Aryan class system, caste discrimination
    b. Appeal to urban merchants, artisans, landed aristocracy, peasants
    c. Preaching in popular dialects, Prakrits (Buddhist Pali, Jain Ardhamagadhi) vs. Sanskrit, the official Brahmanic language

d. Mendicancy, breaking strongest caste taboos by eating alms
      of cooked food from anyone
   e. Public religious gatherings; monastic orders open to all;
      acceptance of women
3. Non-Vedic features; hypothesis of bases in indigenous Indian
   culture
   a. Primitive cult elements, local deities, funeral mounds, tree
      worship
   b. Ahimsa: non-injury to all creatures, unity of life, magic-
      ritualistic taboo against taking any life; cf. primitive totem
      taboo
   c. Belief in transmigration (samsara) based on volitional ac-
      tion (karma); cf. primitive conception of obligatory return
      of departed individual to animal totem, vs. Upanishadic
      conception of binding action, unrelated to rebirth
   d. Recognition of worldly pain in terms of transmigration
      and transitoriness; revelation of remedy
   e. Emancipation in realization of universal truth; abandon-
      ment of phenomenal personality

Reading Assignments

Kosambi, *Ancient India,* 96–114
Thapar, *History of India,* 50–69
Sources of Indian Tradition, 37–72, 93–127; paperback, 35–69, 90–
   124

Optional Assignment

Sources of Indian Tradition, 73–92, 127–153; paperback, 70–89, 124–
   150

Additional Readings

Conze, Edward. *Buddhism: Its Essence and Development.* Oxford:
   Cassirer, 1951. Harper Torchbook paperback, 1959. A sympathetic
   introduction to concepts and practices common to various forms
   of Buddhism.
Conze, Edward. *Buddhist Thought in India.* London: Allen and
   Unwin, 1962. A history of major phases and concepts of Buddhist
   philosophy between 500 B.C. and A.D. 600 in India.
Rahula, Walpola. *What the Buddha Taught.* New York: Grove
   Press, Evergreen paperback, 1959. A good introduction to Pali
   Buddhism by a contemporary Ceylonese Buddhist monk and
   scholar.

Schubring, Walther. *The Doctrine of the Jainas*. Translated by W. Beurlen. Delhi: Motilal Banarsidass, 1962. A translation from the German of an authoritative philological study of Jain thought.

Warren, H.C. (tr.). *Buddhism in Translations: Passages Selected from the Buddhist Sacred Books*. Cambridge: Harvard University Press, 1896. Reprint, 1953. Atheneum paperback, 1963. Excellent translations of well-selected passages from the Pali texts; thematic arrangement of materials introduces the essentials of early Buddhist thought.

For further bibliography and topics on Theravada Buddhism, see de Bary and Embree, *A Guide to Oriental Classics*. New York: Columbia University Press, 1964, 69–77.

Discussion Topics and Questions

1. The significance of scale of urbanization, population levels, agriculture, and material culture in the Middle Ganges (ca. 500 B.C.) in the development of heterodox thought. Compare with earlier urbanization, population levels, agriculture, and material culture of the Indus and Upper Ganges.
2. The popular and philosophical appeals of Jainism and Buddhism in the Indian context of various times; limitations.
3. Nature of the relations between Brahman orthodoxy and Budhists.
4. Compare the legendary lives of Buddha and Mahavira with episodes in the life of Christ: the ideal man, the teacher as savior.
5. Implications of ahimsa as a doctrine of practical ethics.
6. The significance of "suffering" in Buddhist analysis; its relation to transmigration, action.
7. Is Jainism fundamentally pessimistic? Is Buddhism?
8. What are the worldly implications of Jain and Buddhist thought?

VII. MAURYAN EMPIRE: ASCENDANCY AND DISINTEGRATION

(ca. 321–187 B.C.)

A. Sources
   1. Historical records of Greek and Latin writers
   2. Ashokan inscriptions
   3. Coins

4. Archaeological sites
5. Texts: Buddhist Pali Canon, Jain sutras, Sanskrit Epics and Puranas, *Arthaśāstra*
B. Historical background
1. Northwest: foreign influences
  a. Achaemenian empire in Persia (sixth century B.C.); inscriptions mention satrapies in Indus region
  b. Alexander of Macedon's conquest of Punjab (327–325 B.C.); rigors of climate, army mutiny, departure
    1) Political units in northwest defeated, then temporarily welded by Alexander; power vacuum after his departure
    2) Lines of communication between India and the West (Near East, Greece): colonies, trade, diplomacy; Greek coinage, astronomy, and art, Aramaic script, Persian architecture and designs to India; tales of India's fabulous wealth
2. Ganges Basin: consolidation of monarchical power
  a. Kingdoms of sixth to fifth centuries B.C.; Magadhan ascendancy, Kings Bimbasara, Ajatashatru
  b. Nanda dynasty (ca. 362–322 B.C.)
    1) Extension of Magadhan dominion eastward
    2) Power to replenish treasury, maintain huge army; based on agrarian economy: food and goods produced for king and his agents in and around capital; land taxes; trade taxes; tribute
    3) Canals, irrigation projects to increase agricultural productivity
  c. Territorial foundations of empire
    1) Chandragupta, protégé of Taxila Brahman Kautilya ("Indian Machiavelli"); usurped Nanda throne (ca. 322 B.C.); capital Pataliputra
      a) Control of Ganges Plain, Malwa, Kathiawar
      b) Victories over Alexander's prefects in Indus Valley; war with Greek General Seleukos: treaty ceded part of Kabul Valley, cemented by marriage, diplomatic relations
    2) Bindusara, succeeded father ca. 300 B.C.; had extended Mauryan suzerainty over subcontinent by the time he died (ca. 273 B.C.)
D. The reign of Ashoka (ca. 269–232 B.C.): experiment in imperial government

1. Acquisition of power
   a. Fratricidal struggle for throne (ca. 273–269 B.C.)
   b. Kalinga War (260 B.C.); subjugation of hostile east coast; remorse for bloodshed, attraction to Buddhism
2. Dharmavijaya (conquest by "morality"): attempt to bind king and subjects under universal moral law; vs. class, caste, sectarian, regional differences and administrative strains of vast empire
   a. Dharma, focus of unification, intentionally made ambiguous: law, religion, righteous behavior, social order; strongly Buddhist in content
   b. Political and social philosophy of "toleration," plea for suppression of self-interest
   c. Nonviolence: renunciation of conquest by war, abolition of hunting
   d. Edict pillars and rocks: proclamations of dharma engraved in local scripts, local dialects of Prakrit
   e. Officers of dharma employed in capital, towns, territories to oversee public welfare and moral uplift; also foreign envoys, Buddhist missionaries
3. Complex centralized bureaucracy operating in and around Middle Ganges cities, based on efficient collection of agricultural taxes and organization of land in this region
   a. Central power concentrated in king himself
      1) Elaborate espionage system for gathering public opinion and effecting control
      2) Personal travel throughout realm
      3) Role as head of judiciary, military
      4) Blurred distinction between collection of land tax and ownership; king essentially "owned" land
   b. Civil administration
      1) Council of Ministers, including high priest, heir apparent, commander-in-chief
      2) City administrators
      3) District judges; revenue and survey officers
      4) Provincial police, tax collectors
      5) Clerks, scribes, reporters
   c. Military elaborate despite dharmavijaya
   d. State revenue sources
      1) Village lands: king's share, official's share of produce
      2) Cattle from herdsmen
      3) Tribute and prescribed service from artisans

25

       4) Urban areas: birth and death taxes, fines and tithes on sales

    4. Failure of the imperial system

      a. Ashoka's obsession with dharma in later years

        1) Inactive military demoralized

        2) Administrative officers turned into preachers

        3) Unchecked autonomy and corruption of provincial officials

      b. Overburdened economy

      c. Social diversity: loyalty to state and king diffused by family, caste, community, etc.

      d. Ashoka's death led to divided patrimony, weak princes

Reading Assignments

Kosambi, *Ancient India,* 133–65
Thapar, *History of India,* 70–91
Sources of Indian Tradition, 145–53, 236–57; paperback, 142–50, 231–52

Optional Assignment

Wheeler, Mortimer. *Civilizations of the Indus Valley and Beyond.* See III above. Pp. 104–24 deal with evidence of the Mauryan period.

Additional Readings

Majumdar, R.C. (ed.). *The History and Culture of the Indian People.* Volume two, *The Age of Imperial Unity.* Bombay, Bharatiya Vidya Bhavan, 1951. The Mauryan Empire; its predecessors and successors.

Nikam, N.A. and Richard McKeon (ed. and tr.). *The Edicts of Asoka.* Chicago: University of Chicago Press, 1959. Paperback, 1966. Good translations of the known edicts with informative commentary.

Shamasastry, R. (tr.). *Kauṭilya's Arthaśāstra.* Fifth edition. Mysore: Sri Raghuveer Printing Press, 1956. Standard translation of the "Science of Polity" attributed to Chandragupta Maurya's chief minister; primary source of information about the Mauryan administrative system.

Smith, Vincent A. *Asoka, The Buddhist Emperor of India.* Revised edition. Delhi: C. Chand, 1957. Oxford: Clarendon Press, 1901. A somewhat dated but substantial account of the Mauryan ruler and his times; includes translations of the edicts.

Thapar, Romila. *Aśoka and the Decline of the Mauryans.* London: Oxford University Press, 1961. A review and appraisal of historical evidence relating to Ashoka and his period.

Van Buitenen, J.A.B. (tr.). "The Minister's Seal" in *Two Plays of Ancient India.* New York: Columbia University Press, 1968. A semihistorical drama ascribed to Prince Vishakhadatta (sixth century A.D.), set in the court of Chandragupta Maurya; centers on the political schemes of Chanakya (Kautilya), the king's Machiavellian minister. Excellent translation and notes.

Discussion Topics and Questions

1. The Buddhist notion of contractual relation between king and people; Ashoka as a Buddhist emperor and universal king (chakravartin). Evidence of difficulties in effecting state administration on the basis of the Buddhistic concept of dharmavijaya.
2. In what ways was Ashoka's dharmavijaya repressive? Consider specific local and communal factors which militated against imperial unity in Mauryan times.
3. Ashoka's lasting influence in India: dharma in law and politics, Sarnath lion capital as the Indian national symbol.

VIII. POLITICAL FRAGMENTATION AND SYNCRETIC RELIGION

(Second Century B.C. to Third Century A.D.)

A. Mauryan successors
  1. Magadha: Shunga dynasty founded by rebel Mauryan general Pushyamitra (ca. 187–151 B.C.)
    a. Brahmanic reaction to Buddhism
    b. Overthrow by Brahman ministerial family, Kanvas (ca. 75–30 B.C.)
  2. Deccan: Satavahana dynasty (first century B.C. to third century A.D.)
    a. Extensive royal epigraphs; coin hoards
    b. Official support of Brahman orthodoxy
    c. Flourishing Buddhist culture: carved stupas (relic shrines) of Amaravati, etc.
  3. Kalinga: Chedi dynasty, King Kharavela (first century B.C.) avenger of the Mauryan humiliation

4. Tamilnad: Chola, Pandya, Chera kingdoms vie for power; Tamil Sangam literature

B. Foreign invaders in the Northwest
  1. Bactrian Greek and Parthian kings (second to first centuries B.C.); e.g. Greek Menander (155–130 B.C.)
  2. Central Asian nomadic tribes
    a. Shakas driven south by Yueh-chi horde (first century A.D.)
      1) Search for new pastures
      2) Strengthening of Great Wall by Han China
    b. Yueh-chi settlement in Oxus Valley
    c. Ascendancy of Kushana sept under Kujula Kadphises; consolidation of power in Indian borderlands
  3. Kushana monarchy: Indo-Scythian culture (ca. 78–220 A.D.)
    a. Vima Kadphises penetrates India
      1) Abundant gold coinage: Indian influence, Shiva images
      2) Supremacy in Indus and Ganges Basins (to Banaras); Shaka satraps in Western India and Malwa
      3) War with China: defeat, tribute, missions
    b. Kanishka I (reigned first or second century A.D.)
      1) Puzzle of Kushana dates rests on year of accession; theories range from 78–144 A.D.
      2) Dominions in India, Central Asia
        a) North India controlled from Indus capital, Peshawar; Ganges capital, Mathura
        b) Successful wars with Parthians and Chinese in Turkestan and Khotan
      3) Personal religion of Zoroastrian, Greek, Mithraic, Indian gods depicted on coins
      4) Patronage of Buddhism
        a) Development and spread of Mahayana; Chinese, Roman, Persian contacts
        b) Gandhara ("Graeco-Buddhist"), Mathura sculpture styles; Buddha images
        c) Court writers: Nagarjuna, Ashvagosha
    c. Diminished Kushana power continues to third century A.D.: Hinduization of the invaders

C. Mercantile activity
  1. Overland and sea trade with Western and Central Asia, Mediterranean, Southeast Asia, China
  2. Complex cross-cultural communications
  3. Growth of urban artisan guilds
    a. Patronage of Buddhism, Jainism
    b. Centers of technical education

D. Schism in Buddhism: Theravada and Mahayana
  1. Doctrinal disputes, councils, cults, theism after Buddha's death culminate in development of Mahayana ("great vehicle" vs. orthodox Hinayana, "lesser vehicle") first to second centuries A.D.
    a. Buddha the teacher now worshipped as God
    b. Bodhisattva (enlightened being), first used of Buddha in previous incarnations (in Jataka tales)
      1) Bodhisattva seeks enlightenment to enlighten others (vs. selfish Arhat); new stress on compassion: forgoes nirvana to work for salvation of all sufferers
      2) New ideal: Buddhahood for all
    c. Popular level: salvation through worship of heavenly savior Buddhas and Bodhisattvas, divine grace, merit, and devotion
  2. Scholastic philosophic traditions
    a. Theravada
      1) Abhidhamma: psychological and metaphysical doctrines of Pali canon
      2) *Milindapañha, (Questions of King Menander)*: dialogue between Greek king and Buddhist monk
    b. Mahayana
      1) Madhyamika (Doctrine of the "Middle Way"); Nagarjuna (first to second century A.D.), doctrine of emptiness (Shunyavada): understanding meaninglessness of transmigration, etc.; middle way between existence and and nonexistence; dialectic of negation; use of reason to defeat itself; meditation
      2) Vijnanavada (Doctrine of Consciousness); Asanga, Vasubandhu (fourth century A.D.): pure idealism
      3) Logic; Dignaga, Dharmakirti
  3. Diffusion of Buddhism: world religion
    a. Missionary activities, monastic rule, monk's mobility, welfare projects, universities, e.g. Nalanda
    b. Support of kings, merchants, guilds; patronage of Ashoka, Kanishka
    c. Theravada spread within India, Ceylon; with trade to Burma, Siam, Southeast Asia
    d. Mahayana carried to Central Asia, China
F. Brahmanic syncretism
  1. Impact of heterodoxies
    a. Modifications of Vedic sacrifices, gods
    b. Notions of compassionate deity

c. Concept of cyclic creation
2. Sectarian monotheism
   a. Vishnu: descent in various forms in times of evil to save man, e.g. Krishna
   b. Shiva: incorporates elements of ancient fertility gods, worshipped as phallus (lingam)
3. Devotionalism: personal relationship between god and devotee (bhakti)
4. Sanctification and revision of the Epics; many sectarian interpolations, e.g. *Bhagavad Gītā* (ca. 100 B.C.–A.D. 100)
   a. Deification of mythic hero of Yadava tribe, Krishna, as supreme God, incarnation of Vishnu, man's teacher (guru)
   b. Discourse between charioteer Krishna and warrior Arjuna on Kurukshetra battlefield
      1) Arjuna: why fight? why function in the world?
      2) Krishna: pure duty; work (karma) to keep order (dharma) just as I, God, work to keep order, without attachment to the fruits of work; sacrifice = devotion (bhakti) to God = freedom from the bondage of work = freedom from transmigration (samsara), the Indian religious ideal
   c. Syncretic religio-philosophical text: Krishna expounds every contemporary philosophy in turn, all views of One God, many disciplines (yoga) or ways to salvation
      1) Analysis (sankhya): based on matter/spirit dualism
      2) Work (karma): all action as sacrifice to Krishna, reinterpretation of old Vedic sacrifice
      3) Knowledge (jnana): in Upanishadic mystical sense
      4) Devotion (bhakti): surrender to god = sacrifice = union with God; major point of *Gītā*

Reading Assignments

Kosambi, *Ancient India,* 166–92
Thapar, *History of India,* 92–135
Sources of Indian Tradition, 154–202; paperback, 151–99

Optional Assignment

Zaehner, R.C. (ed. and tr.). *Hindu Scriptures.* See IV above. Pp. 249–325 include the entire *Bhagavad Gītā.*

Additional Readings

Cowell, E.B., F.M. Müller, and J. Takakusu (trs.). *Buddhist Mahayana Texts.* Sacred Books of the East, volume 49. Oxford: Clarendon Press, 1894. Dover paperback, 1969. A collection of basic Mahayana texts, including Ashvagosha's *Life of Buddha* and *The Diamond Sutra*.

Edgerton, Franklin. *The Bhagavad Gītā*. Harvard Oriental Series, volumes 38–39. Transliterated Sanskrit text, translation, and a series of short critical essays on the background, philosophy, and religion of the *Gītā*.

Leeuw, von Lohuizen de. *The Scythian Period*. Leiden: E.J. Brill, 1949. A somewhat technical but fascinating study of the origins, chronology, and culture of the Indo-Scythians.

Majumdar, R.C. (ed.). *The History and Culture of the Indian People*. Volume two, *The Age of Imperial Unity*. See IV above. Much of this volume deals with the Mauryan successors and foreign invaders of the period.

Nilakanta Shastri, K.A. *A History of South India*. Second edition. Revised. London: Oxford University Press, 1958. A survey of South Indian history; places post-Mauryan dynasties in context of region.

Rowland, Benjamin. *The Art and Architecture of India*. Baltimore: Penguin Books, 1953. Chapters 6–14, 20–24 survey Buddhist art in India, Central Asia, Ceylon, and Southeast Asia; well illustrated.

Suzuki, D.T. *On Indian Mahayana Buddhism*. Edited with an introduction by Edward Conze. New York: Harper Torchbooks paperback, 1968. A collection of the writings of the renowned Zen scholar on Indian Mahayana; valuable for their presentation of philosophical developments in terms of Buddhist life and meditational experience.

Tarn, William N. *The Greeks in Bactria and India*. Revised edition. Cambridge: Cambridge University Press, 1951. Reconstruction of the history of Greek kingdoms in India following Mauryan decline. (Interpretations revised by numismatic evidence in A.K. Narain, *The Indo-Greeks*. Oxford: Clarendon Press, 1957.)

For further bibliography and topics on texts of Mahayana Buddhism and on the *Bhagavad Gītā*, see de Bary and Embree, *A Guide to Oriental Classics*. New York: Columbia University Press, 1964, 78–85 and 52–56.

Discussion Topics and Questions

1. Examples of architecture and sculpture from the Shunga, Satavahana, Kushana periods as evidence of developments in the religion and material culture of the times.
2. Contributions of the Central Asian invaders to Indian civilization.

3. Significance of foreign trade in the development of Indian economy, politics, religion, art.
4. Conceptions of Buddha in Theravada, popular Mahayana, philosophical Mahayana.
5. Cultural significance of the Mahayana religious ideal.
6. Fundamental ways in which the religion Krishna preaches in the *Bhagavad Gītā* differs from that of the Upanishads, Jainism, and Buddhism.
7. Krishna's answer to Arjuna's concern with the social consequences of war.

IX. GUPTA PERIOD: INDIAN CLASSICISM
(ca. 320–647)

A. Gupta dynasty: paramount power (ca. 320–480)
    1. Sources: numerous dated inscriptions, coins, Chinese records
    2. Origin: Magadhan king's marriage alliance with ancient Licchavi tribe
        a. Took historic name Chandragupta
        b. Extended dominion into Kushana vacuum; Pataliputra, capital
        c. Established "Gupta" era, based on accession date ca. 320
    3. Samudragupta (ca. 335–375): imperial ambitions, military campaigns
        a. Annexation and tribute in North, Deccan; weakening of tribal republics
        b. Patronage of Brahmanic Hinduism: Vedic horse sacrifice to assert imperial claim; divine character of kingship
        c. Patronage of literature, music, art
    4. Chandragupta II (ca. 375–415); called Vikramaditya (valor-sun)
        a. Power over Shakas (Northwest), Malwa
        b. Marriage alliances with Deccan dynasties, e.g. Vakatakas
        c. Urban prosperity, mild administration reported by Fa-hsien, Chinese pilgrim (399–414)
        d. Nine "jewels" of learning legends associate with his court include poet Kalidasa
    5. Kumaragupta (ca. 415–455), few extant records
    6. Skandagupta (ca. 455–480): Hun invasions destroy political system and high culture

7. North India divided into four main kingdoms: "Guptas" of Magadha, Maukharis, Pushyabhutis, Maitrakas—rivals for power
B. Hun invaders: Central Asian barbarian hordes spread over Roman Empire and Persia; attacks on Gupta territories
   1. Established in Malwa by ca. 500
   2. Mihirakula: tyrant and iconoclast, known from tradition recorded by Chinese pilgrim Hsuan-tsang and Kashmiri historian Kalhana, inscriptions, coins, etc.
   3. Indian power broken ca. 528 by King Yashodharman of Malwa
C. Harsha of Kanauj (606–647): Gupta revival in Northern India
   1. Sources: Bana's romantic biography *Harṣacarita*, official Chinese historical works, Hsuan-tsang's account, inscriptions, coins
   2. Power base: Pushyabhuti king, united with Maukharis, capital at Kanauj
   3. Control, suzerainty over northern kingdoms; vain campaigns to extend power to Deccan and southern India, defeat by Chalukya king, Pulakeshin II
   4. Scholar and patron of literature; credited with a grammatical work, poems, three Sanskrit plays (two comedies and Buddhist drama)
   5. Patron of religion: devout Shiva worshipper; turned to Buddhism later in reign
   6. Depicted in account of Hsuan-tsang, Chinese pilgrim throughout India (630–643), eight years in Harsha's dominions: ceremonial assemblies at Kanauj and Prayaga (tributary kings; Buddhist, Brahman, Jain theologians; distribution of royal gifts), cultured court, royal control of administration through personal tours
   7. His death left realm in chaos: power struggle among independent states; disunion emerged as political pattern of North India
D. Gupta political institutions: similar to Mauryan but less centralized
   1. Administration based on land revenue
   2. Provincial autonomy
   3. Independent village and city governing bodies, guild organizations
E. Gupta culture
   1. Sanskrit revival

      a. Inscriptions, coin legends

      b. Royal patronage of literature, theatre; e.g. Kalidasa's poems and plays

  2. Scientific writings: mathematics (use of decimal system, zero sign), astronomy, and astrology; Greek influences; Aryabhata's astronomy

  3. Classical climax in painting, sculpture

      a. Ajanta Buddhist cave paintings

      b. Sarnath Buddha images, figures, and reliefs

      c. Deogarh Vishnu temple

  4. Brahmanic renaissance: crystallization of sanatana-dharma (eternal way or religion), Indian phrase for "Hinduism"

F. Classical Hinduism (term "Hindu" given currency by Arabs in eighth century A.D. in reference to followers of prevailing Indian religion, either Shiva or Vishnu sectarians)

  1. Brahmanism, influenced by ideas current in early centuries A.D., assumed religious features which still distinguish "Hinduism"

      a. Not founded by historical personage; grew and evolved from a variety of cults and beliefs; flexibility and continuity

          1) Foundations in Vedic religion

          2) Popular cults continually absorbed

      b. Way of life; not divorced from everyday existence

  2. Characterizing elements

      a. Spiritual teacher (guru), e.g. Krishna/Arjuna

      b. Philosophic inquiry (darshana); means to find Truth, which is salvation (moksha)

      c. Practical path (sadhana); preparation through moral, devotional disciplines

      d. Relativity of aspirants' potentialities: variety of paths, levels of truth, "tolerance"

      e. Equilibrium (samya), avoidance of extremes

      f. Organization of life, to reconcile diverse aspects

          1) Duties of social rank and stages of life (varnashrama-dharma)

             a) Ranks (varnas): priest, warrior, everyman, servant

             b) Stages (ashramas): celibate student, householder, forest dweller, wandering ascetic

          2) Ends of man (purushartha), legitimate pursuits

             a) Three worldly aims: social responsibility (dharma), material and political success (artha), aesthetic and erotic pleasure (kama)

b) Extra-mundane aim: salvation (moksha)
g. Vaishnava and Shaiva sectarianism

Reading Assignments

Thapar, *History of India,* 136–66
Sources of Indian Tradition, 203–75; paperback, 200–70

Optional Assignment

Rowland, Benjamin. *The Ajanta Caves: Early Buddhist Painting from India.* New York: Mentor-UNESCO Art Book, 1963. A volume of color reproductions, with introduction.

Additional Readings

Bana. *Harṣacarita.* Translated by E.B. Cowell and F.W. Thomas. Reprint. Delhi: Motilal Banarsidass, 1961. London: Royal Asiatic Society, 1897. Earliest example of historical romance in Sanskrit; often tedious but informative.

Beal, Samuel (tr.). *Chinese Accounts of India.* Four volumes. Calcutta: Sushil Gupta, 1958. Reprint of Beal's *Si-Yu-Ki: Buddhist Records of the Western World.* London: Kegan, Paul, Trench, and Trubner, 1884. Incorporates the records of various early Chinese Buddhist pilgrims, including Hsuan-tsang's account of India during the reign of Harsha. Thomas Watters' translation, entitled *On Yüan Chwang's Travels in India* (Two *volumes.* London: Royal Asiatic Society, 1904–1905), is a more authoritative version of Hsuan-tsang.

Kramrisch, Stella. *The Hindu Temple.* Two volumes. Calcutta: Calcutta University, 1946. Stimulating depth study of the Hindu temple, which became central to developing Hinduism in Gupta times; superbly illustrated.

Lal, P. (tr.). *Great Sanskrit Plays in Modern Translation.* Norfolk, Connecticut: New Directions, 1964. Cloth and paperback. Enjoyable English "transcreations" of classical plays; read togther, they give a feeling for courtly and upper-class life in the Gupta period, when patronage of such drama flourished. Also, Van Buitenen, *Two Plays of Ancient India;* see VII above.

Majumdar, R.C. (ed.). *History and Culture of the Indian People.* Volume III, *The Classical Age,* chapters I–IX. See IV above. The Gupta period and the reign of Harsha of Kanauj.

Renou, Louis. *Religions of Ancient India.* London: Athlone Press, 1953. Schocken paperback, 1968. The portion on Hinduism (46–110), attempts to define the essentials of Indian religion.

Rowland, Benjamin. *The Art and Architecture of India*. Baltimore: Penguin Books, 1953. Chapter 15 introduces the art of the Gupta Age; well illustrated.

Discussion Topics and Questions

1. The meaning of "classical"; its application to Gupta India.
2. The king as patron of art and religion as well as general, chief executive, judge; political and cultural implications.
3. Urban, court, and country life as depicted in contemporaneous art, drama, biography, and travel records.
4. Gupta evidence of strains in Indian culture which counter the undertone of pessimistic world despair; sorrow as a theological presupposition (cf. original sin) vs. everyday life and religion.
5. The role of the Brahman priest and lawgiver in developing Hinduism vs. Vedic religion.

X. TRADITIONAL HINDU SOCIETY: "CASTE" AND "CLASS"

A. Conflicting Sources: contextual vs. textual
   1. Village social organization in operation: complexity and regional variability, observations based mainly on contemporary village studies
   2. Brahmanical law books (ca. 200 B.C.–A.D. 200): codification and valuation of social relationships in terms of theoretical structure; e.g. *Manusmṛti;* descriptions of ideal social structure, Brahmanic view of the way society *should* be
B. Problems of terminology
   1. "Caste" from Portugese "casta" (breed) refers to jati (birth group, genus)
   2. Confusion in nomenclature for social structures reflects conflicting views of the origin of the caste system and caste proliferation
      a. "Four castes" (varna), "subcastes" (jati): based on Brahmanic theory of caste origins from fission of four classes
      b. "Castes" (jati) vs. "classes" or "ranks" (varna): based on literary and anthropological evidence for complex social and economic background of caste origin and proliferation; ranking system often sanctifies secular differences
C. Caste system, jati: operative social structure
   1. Similar structure throughout most of India; regional variation in forms, terms

2. Group exclusiveness: coexistence of diverse behavioral patterns in terms of family organization, gods, worship, work, food, garments
   a. Different origins: importance of local and immigrant tribes
   b. Varied times of settlement in region
   c. Economic and ritual specialization according to local need
3. Social, economic, and religious manifestations of caste
   a. Endogamy; caste as extended family, kinship entity, marriage circle
   b. Commensality
   c. Regional limits, generally linguistic boundaries
   d. Hereditary occupation; extreme specialization in rural as well as urban society
   e. Traditional pattern of mutual duties, rights; enforced by internal agency (caste council)
   f. Hierarchical position in relation to other castes; ranking order by majority acceptance in small area (village, region); considerable disagreement on rank; group mobility
      1) Ritual status: preparation and distribution of food, consumption of food at festivals, pollution and purity taboos
      2) Economic position: within jajmani system (see XI. C. 5. below); extra-jajmani contractual relationships; personal attributes, such as land and wealth, acquisition or loss of which may affect rank
D. System of classes or ranks, varna: ideal social structure
   1. Theoretical ranking of caste groups in four broadly occupational divisions by Brahman lawgivers
      a. Based on three-fold Aryan social order: Brahman (priest), Kshatriya (warrior), Vaishya (member of community)
         1) All "twice-born," initiated with sacred thread
         2) Common gods, ritual
      b. Fourth rank: Shudra
         1) Functions to serve "twice-born"; no rights to Aryan ritual
         2) Contains majority of caste groups, especially craftsmen and performers of services; laborers, agriculturalists, and landowners also represented
   2. Exterior or "untouchable" castes: pariahs (Tamil *paraiyan*, literally "drummer"); sometimes called the fifth rank (panchama), includes most of unskilled laborers, e.g. field laborers, scavengers; also low rank skilled occupations, e.g. leatherworkers

37

3. Religious justifications of privilege; legitimization of upper caste exploitation
   a. Dharma: cosmic order, social law, code of rights and duties
   b. Vrata: function, individual conduct (in terms of group membership)
   c. Karma: action, work—its retribution and reward
4. "Sanskritization" (Srinivas): imitation of higher status by groups striving for symbolic justification of better social position; "elite emulation" (Owen M. Lynch)
   a. Nature of claims, appeals to Brahmanic law
   b. Effects on the established order

Reading Assignments

Cohn, *India: Social Anthropology,* 111–41
Kosambi, *Ancient India,* 14–16, 166–76
Srinivas, M.N. "Sanskritization," in *Social Change in Modern India.* Berkeley: University of California Press, 1968. Paperback, 1970. Pp. 1–45. The chapter on Sanskritization analyzes the processes by which institutions, rites, myths, and values of status Hinduism have been spread to various levels of Indian culture.

Optional Assignments

Beals, Alan. *Gopalpur: A South Indian Village.* New York: Holt, Rinehart and Winston paperback, 1966. An anthropological case study of a traditional village in Mysore; emphasis is given to the interpersonal relationships which constitute village life. Chapters 3–4 deal with caste in a South Indian village.
Lewis, Oscar. *Village Life in Northern India: Studies in a Delhi Village.* Urbana: University of Illinois Press, 1958. New York: Random House, Vintage paperback, 1965. Presentation and analysis of basic features of traditional Indian peasant society; a problem-oriented study of a particular village. Chapter 2 deals with caste in a North Indian village.

Additional Readings

Bailey, Frederick G. *Nation, Caste, and Tribe.* Manchester: University of Manchester Press, 1960. A study of changes affecting the Kond tribal people of Orissa as a result of contact with Hindu peasant neighbors and government.
Bühler, Georg (tr.). *The Laws of Manu.* Sacred Books of the East, volume 25. Oxford: Clarendon Press, 1886. Many reprints. Earliest

of the Brahmanic lawbooks; detailed manual of human conduct composed from Brahman viewpoint.

Cox, Oliver C. *Caste, Class and Race: A Study in Social Dynamics.* New York: Doubleday, 1948. New York Monthly Review Press paperback, 1970. A socioeconomic analysis of concepts of caste, class, and race relations in various societies; with concluding discussion on race in the United States.

De Reuck, Anthony, and Julie Knight. *Caste and Race: Comparative Approaches.* Boston: Little, Brown, 1967. A CIBA Foundation symposium on the nature of caste segregation and racist ideologies, drawing on studies of Indian, Japanese, American, and European societies.

Hutton, John H. *Caste in India.* Fourth edition. London: Oxford University Press, 1963. A comprehensive survey discussing the history, nature, and function of caste.

Hsu, Francis L.K. *Clan, Caste, and Club.* Princeton: D. Van Nostrand paperback, 1963. A comparative study of Chinese, Hindu, and American societies through analysis of typical groups in each culture.

India (Republic). *The Adivasis.* New Delhi: Publications Division, Ministry of Information and Broadcasting, Government of India, 1960. A survey of tribal groups in India.

Karve, Irawati. *Hindu Society—An Interpretation.* Poona: Deccan College, 1961. An interpretation of the historical development and characteristic features of the caste system viewed as an integrating social structure.

Karve, Irawati. *Kinship in India.* Poona: Deccan College, 1953. A regional survey of kinship systems; variations are related to geographical and linguistic factors.

Lynch, Owen M. *The Politics of Untouchability: Social Mobility and Social Change in a City of India.* New York: Columbia University Press, 1969. An anthropologist's study of a community of leatherworkers living in Agra; stresses the complexity of social change in contemporary urban India.

Mandelbaum, David G. *Society in India.* Volume one, *Community and Change.* Volume two, *Change and Continuity.* Berkeley: University of California Press paperback, 1970. A comprehensive study of Indian social relations in terms of the changing social systems to which they belong; includes analyses of subcontinental patterns of social relations, as well as group and regional variations.

Mayer, Adrian C. *Caste and Kinship in Central India.* Berkeley:

University of California Press, 1960. Paperback, 1970. A detailed study of various aspects of caste as practiced in a particular locality.

Silverberg, James (ed.). *Social Mobility in the Caste System in India: An Interdisciplinary Symposium.* The Hague: Mouton, 1968. Challenges to many long-standing notions about social immobility are presented from different points of view.

Singer, Milton (ed.). *Traditional India: Structure and Change.* Philadelphia: American Folklore Society, 1959. Includes an excellent set of articles on the traditions of the different classes in Hindu society.

Singer, Milton, and Bernard S. Cohen. *Structure and Change in Indian Society.* Chicago: Aldine, 1968. Essays by outstanding scholars demonstrating recent theoretical and methodological innovations in the anthropological analysis of Indian social structure and social change.

Discussion Topics and Questions

1. In what ways does a caste (jati) differ from a tribe, guild, clan, social class?
2. What are the economic bases of the caste system?
3. Account for the endurance of the caste system. What advantages does such a society offer and to whom? Disadvantages?
4. To what extent is the varna model a meaningful factor of Hindu society? How does it reflect Aryan accommodation to the indigenous system?
5. How alterable is a man's position in traditional Indian society? What are the vehicles of mobility? What retards social change?

XI. URBAN AND RURAL INDIA

A. Similarity in ancient and modern circumstances
   1. Geographic factors determine settlement patterns: land, water, transportation
   2. Population distribution: India still over 80 percent rural
   3. Social organization: community separation
      a. Members of each caste, craft, religion, language, race generally live together in segregated neighborhoods
      b. Modification in cosmopolitan centers
B. Cities of ancient and classical India

1. Centers expressive of formalized "high" culture; arts, learning, institutionalized dissent, foreign contacts
2. Several primary functions, often overlapping
    a. Administrative center, royal capital; e.g. Hastinapur, Pataliputra, Peshawar, Kanauj
    b. Religious center
        1) Pilgrimage site; e.g. Kashi (Banaras—River Ganges, Sarnath Deer Park), Prayag (Allahabad), Gaya, Puri, Shrirangam, Madura
        2) Seat of learning; e.g. Nalanda, Buddhist university, attracted foreign students
    c. Commercial center, trade depot; e.g. Madura, Takshashila (Taxila), Ujjayini
3. Heterogeneous inhabitants; population density
    a. Merchants, government officials, intellectuals, princes, priests, monks, courtesans, artisans, entertainers, servants
    b. Concentrations of educated, prosperous, discontented, dispossessed people: basis for religious, social, political innovation
4. Money and barter economy based on commerce: the search for profit and worldly success (artha)
    a. Industry and trade
    b. Banking
5. Craft guilds: organize production, dominate urban commercial relations, e.g. potters, metal workers, carpenters
    a. Caste associations provide continuity
    b. Donations to religious institutions for charitable works, buildings, art
6. Refined aesthetic life: the pursuit of pleasure (kama)
    a. Appreciation and practice of music, poetry, painting
    b. Cultivation of the art of love: the accomplished courtesan; Vatsyayana's *Kāmasūtra*
C. The Indian village
    1. No "typical" village
        a. Examples illustrate general pattern and variations
        b. Life determined by many variables: regional setting, income, castes, etc.; broad north-south contrasts in village forms, houses, diet, festivals, marriage systems (see Lewis, Beals)
    2. Nucleated and non-nucleated settlement patterns
        a. Origins
            1) Defense

41

2) Water supply and storage in monsoon and arid climates: public wells, tanks, irrigation projects
    b. Relative autonomy; the myth of self-sufficiency
        1) Direct or indirect economic dependence on village lands
        2) Internal power hierarchy, service relationships, gods, festivals, shrines
        3) Exploitation of low-ranking castes
        4) Cultural backwater: social, economic stagnation
3. Agricultural economy: mainly subsistence farming, regional and local variability
    a. Land: quality, quantity, tenure (communal vs. private holdings), fragmentation, irrigation
    b. Crops: growing seasons, food and cash crops
    c. Tools and equipment: requirements for dry and wet cultivation, specialty crops
    d. Cultivation methods: ploughing, sowing, harvesting
    e. Livestock: draft work, dairy products, dung for fertilizer and fuel
    f. Human labor: small owners, tenants, landless; group specialization in terms of caste
4. Social fragmentation of groups: caste system (detailed above)
    a. Spatial separation of castes dominates village plan
    b. Land ownership and social hierarchy reflect fragmentation
5. Economic interaction of groups in production and exchange of goods and services
    a. "Jajmani system" widespread kind of system, with regional variability: "Under this system each caste group within a village is expected to give certain standardized services to families of another caste" (Lewis)
        1) Hereditary relations: jajman = recipient of service: kamin = performer of service
        2) Kamins receive food, clothing, cash from landowners for obligatory performance of occupational and ceremonial services; also, exchange of services
        3) System favors landed; crisis assistance for kamins assured
    b. Non-jajmani relationships: cash/kind payments for less essential craft goods and skilled services; also seasonal field laborers
    c. "Malnad system" (Edward B. Harper), villages operating fundamentally on cash basis, without permanent and heritable economic alliances; based on cash crop production, medium of exchange which fluctuates in value

6. Village Hinduism: local cults and deities mixed with Brahmanic scriptural tradition
   a. Tutelary and fertility deities given orthodox trappings; scriptural gods have local characteristics
   b. Worship includes festival cycles of local ceremonies and regional celebrations, as well as Sanskritic rituals and cult rites
   c. Village shamans deal with individuals' needs; Brahman priesthood concerned with maintenance of cosmic and social order
   d. Hybrid imagery of village shrines and temples
7. Beyond the village: broader contexts
   a. Social institutions
      1) Village exogamy
      2) Caste ties in neighboring villages
   b. Economic exchanges
      1) Inter-village service relationships; itinerant artisans, specialists (astrologers, doctors), peddlers
      2) Periodic bazaars in larger villages and towns; daily produce markets
      3) Administration: taxation, courts, land records, etc.
   c. Religious and cultural traditions
      1) Textual sources for Brahman priests and literati
      2) Pilgrimages, temples
      3) Itinerant bards, musicians, actors
      4) Inter-village and regional festivals

Reading Assignments

Cohn, *India: Social Anthropology,* 142–56
Kosambi, *Ancient India,* 16–22, 192–98
Thapar, *History of India,* review 109–13

Optional Assignments

Beals, Alan R. *Gopalpur: A South Indian Village.* See X above.
Lewis, Oscar. *Village Life in Northern India: Studies in a Delhi Village.* See X above.
Van Buitenen, J.A.B. (tr.). *Tales of Ancient India.* Chicago: University of Chicago Press, 1959. New York: Bantam paperback, 1961. The tales, drawn from several sources, offer insight into the secular life and concerns of urban society in classical India.
Wheeler, Mortimer. *Civilizations of the Indus Valley and Beyond.* See III above; review descriptions of ancient cities.

Wolf, Eric R. *Peasants*. See II above; review with attention to the relations between the rural populations and the complex society outside the village.

Additional Readings

Beidelman, Thomas O. *A Comparative Analysis of the Hindu Jajmani System*. Monographs of the Association for Asian Studies, volume VIII. Locust Valley, New York: Augustin, 1959. A review of the literature on India's major village socioeconomic system.

Berreman, Gerald D. *Hindus of the Himalayas*. Berkeley: University of California Press, 1963. Ethnographic account based on a village study in the Pahari-speaking region of North India, with emphasis on regional social and economic features.

Bose, Nirmal Kumar. *Peasant Life in India*. Calcutta: The Anthropological Survey of India, 1962. An illustrated survey of the material culture of the countryside, including village types, food, tools, dress.

Burton, Sir Richard F. (tr.). *The Kama Sutra of Vatsyayana: The Classic Hindu Treatise on Love and Social Conduct*. New York: Dutton, 1962. The best available translation of the famous Indian treatise on erotics; rich source for material on the traditional social life of the prosperous Indian urbanite.

Dube, Shyama C. *Indian Village*. Ithaca: Cornell University Press, 1955. Harper Colophon paperback, 1967. A descriptive analysis of the culture of a village near Hyderabad in the Deccan Plateau, located 100 miles from Gopalpur.

Harper, Edward B. "Two Systems of Economic Exchange in Village India," *American Anthropologist*, 61, no. 5 (October, 1959), 760–78.

Lynch, Owen M. *The Politics of Untouchability: Social Mobility and Social Change in a City of India*. See X above.

Marriott, McKim (ed.). *Village India: Studies in the Little Community*. Chicago: University of Chicago Press, 1955. Paperback, 1969. A collection of papers on aspects of life in villages of different regions; focusing on the position of the "little community" in civilization.

Minturn, Leigh, and John T. Hitchcock. *The Rājpūts of Khalapur, India*. New York: Wiley paperback, 1966. One of a series of studies of childrearing in divergent cultures; description and analysis of the socialization processes operative in a North Indian village.

Rao, Raja. *Kanthapura*. London: Allen and Unwin, 1938. New Directions paperback, 1967. A novel about the impact of the Indian independence movement on a traditional South Indian village, Kanthapura; conveys the social complexity, conservatism, and richness of rural life.

Singer, Milton. "The Great Tradition of Hinduism in the City of Madras," in *Traditional India: Structure and Change*. Philadelphia: American Folklore Society, 1959. Also in Charles Leslie (ed.), *Anthropology of Folk Religion*. New York: Vintage paperback, 1960, 105–66.

Spate, O.H.K. and A.T.A. Learmonth. Revised edition. *India and Pakistan: A General and Regional Geography*. London: Methuen, 1967. See I above. Chapter 7, "Village and Town in India," gives general characteristics of village and town life; urbanization is considered demographically in chapter 4. The great cities and village patterns receive separate treatment in the regional chapters.

Turner, Ray (ed.). *India's Urban Future*. Berkeley: University of California Press, 1962. A collection of essays on problems of urban communities in India; includes a survey of literature on the subject.

Vidyarthi, L.P. *The Sacred Complex in Hindu Gaya*. New York: Asia Publishing House, 1961. A study of a pilgrimage center in Bihar associated with both Vishnu and Buddha; emphasis is on the role of its Brahman ritual specialists.

Discussion Topics and Questions

1. Consider the nature of Indian cities in relation to classical definitions (cf. Fustel de Coulanges, *The Ancient City;* Max Weber, *The City*).
2. Compare aspects of Indian spatial segregation with those of the European city and the "ghetto."
3. Compare the values of Indian city dwellers and peasants (Van Buitenen, Beals).
4. Discuss the economic and cultural importance of rural communities and Indian civilization.
5. Compare the position of a low-caste kamin in the jajmani system with that of a Greek or Roman slave, a feudal serf, an indentured servant.
6. Discuss the networks of communication which link villages and cities.

XII. CLASSICAL HINDU PHILOSOPHY: KNOWLEDGE AS POWER

A. Darshana, Sanskrit term for philosophy
  1. Literally "view," "seeing" the nature of reality
  2. Means for destroying ignorance (which is bondage), achieving freedom from limitations of empirical existence
B. Identification and investigation of fundamental problems
  1. Causality: change and continued existence; creation, relation of cause and effect
  2. Individuality: soul and material body; relation to ultimate reality
  3. Knowledge: axiomatic criteria of valid knowledge; idealism vs. realism; nescience, false perception, appearance and reality, levels of truth
  4. Salvation: cosmic union or isolation; release from limiting barriers, total freedom
C. Orthodox systems
  1. Formalizations of Brahmanic responses to Buddhist (also Jain and materialist Charvaka) theories (ca. A.D. 200–800)
  2. Acceptance of divine origin and infallible authority of Vedas
D. Six major schools
  1. Sources: standardized texts of aphorisms and verses, interpretative commentaries by masters
  2. Distinctive positions
    a. Sankhya (analysis, enumeration): dualism of "matter," "environment" (prakriti), and "personality" (purusha); bondage is deluded identification of the two; analysis of generative process in terms of 25 factors; atheistic
    b. Yoga (discipline, cognate of English "yoke"): method for liberation of personality from matter; psycho-physical therapy
    c. Nyaya (logic): epistemological method, knowledge by influence or syllogistic argument (five-member syllogism), as well as Vedic authority, perception, comparison; pluralistic view of reality
    d. Vaisheshika (particularity): pluralistic physics and metaphysics; eternal reality of distinct substances (earth, water, fire, air, ether, time, space, mind, self or atman) and categories
    e. Mimamsa or Karma-mimamsa (investigation, investigation

of action): exegesis of Vedic ritual texts; nature of religious action

 f. Vedanta (end of the Vedas): development out of Upanishadic speculation; philosophers vary on relation of phenomenal diversity and ultimate reality, individuality and supreme being

 3. Yoga meditation and Vedanta metaphysics most enduring, influential within India and abroad

E. Yoga

 1. Meditational tradition of ancient origin, method adopted by various schools of thought, including Buddhism

 2. Basic text: *Yogasūtra* of Patanjali (ca. third century A.D.)

 3. Purpose: involution of evolutionary process (as described in Sankhya), perfect equilibrium; isolation of personality from environment = freedom

 4. Discipline: suppression of mental activity by eightfold process of physical, moral, mental control culminating in trance (samadhi)

F. Vedanta

 1. Prevailing philosophy of India after A.D. 800; medieval and modern popularizations

 2. Basic text: *Vedāntasūtra,* or *Brahmasūtra,* attributed to Badarayana; elliptical aphorisms attempting to systematize Upanishads

 3. Commentaries: numerous interpretations, three major philosophers

  a. Shankara (ca. 780–820): nondualism (advaita)

   1) Ultimate reality (brahman) is unitary, pure intelligence; diversity is illusion (maya); exaggeration of Upanishadic equation atman = brahman

   2) Epistemological emphasis; reliance on scriptural authority and exegisis; false notions of plurality and causality arise from making categories (maya); "superimposition"

   3) God is man's highest representation of reality

   4) Realization of absolute unity = freedom

  b. Ramanuja (ca. 1017–1137): qualified nondualism

   1) Diversity within unity

   2) Theistic emphasis; Vaishnava sectarianism: reconciliation of Hindu theology and devotional cults

   3) One God, many souls; God is ultimate reality (brahman)

4) Pure devotion = direct knowledge of God, by grace; permanent intuition of God = freedom
c. Madhva (ca. 1197–1276): dualism
1) Individuals and world subordinate to and dependent on God
2) God or Brahman identified with Vishnu, director of the world

Reading Assignments

Thapar, *History of India,* 161–63
Sources of Indian Tradition, 300–27; paperback, 295–322

Optional Assignment

Berry, Thomas. *Religions of India: Hinduism, Yoga, Buddhism.* New York: Bruce, 1971. Pp. 75–115 are a sympathetic introduction to Yoga in its various meanings and aspects.

Radhakrishnan, Sarvepalli, and C.A. Moore (eds.). *A Source Book on Indian Philosophy.* Princeton: Princeton University Press, 1957. Paperback, 1967. Pp. 453–85 present a readable translation of Patanjali's *Yogasūtra,* with commentaries. Pp. 506–72 present translations of selections from texts of major Vedanta philosophers. Translations from major texts of each of the six systems are preceded by useful introductory material (349–572).

Additional Readings

Dasgupta, Surendranath. *A History of Indian Philosophy.* Five volumes. Cambridge: Cambridge University Press, 1922–1955. Detailed, technical descriptions and analyses of the Indian philosophical traditions, including systems of Hindu, Buddhist, Jain origin.

Eliade, Mircea. *Yoga: Immortality and Freedom.* Bollingen Series, no. 56. Translated from the French by W.R. Trask. New York: Pantheon, 1958. Interpretive survey of the history, theory, and practice of Yoga.

Potter, Karl H. *Presuppositions of India's Philosophies.* Englewood Cliffs, New Jersey: Prentice-Hall, 1963. An analysis emphasizing attitudes and beliefs that govern Indian speculative thought; presents a topical reclassification of the classical schools of philosophy in terms of key concepts.

Sharma, Chandradhar. *Indian Philosophy: A Critical Survey.* London: Rider, 1960. Barnes and Noble paperback, 1962. A technical but concise historical survey of concepts, systems, and thinkers; includes a glossary of Sanskrit philosophical vocabulary.

Wood, Ernest. *Yoga*. Baltimore: Penguin paperback, 1959. A nontechnical summary of concepts and methods from various systems of spiritual and physical disciplines that were formalized in the Yoga school; frequent reference to Patanjali's *Yogasūtra*.

Zimmer, Heinrich. *Philosophies of India*. Edited by Joseph Campbell. New York: Pantheon, 1951. Meridian paperback, 1956. Well-written and stimulating; valuable if the speculative nature of Zimmer's interpretations is kept in mind.

For further bibliography and topics on Yoga and Advaita Vedanta, see de Bary and Embree, *A Guide to Oriental Classics*. New York: Columbia University Press, 1964, 60–68.

Discussion Topics and Questions

1. Compare dominant ideals of Greek and Indian philosophy, e.g. Platonic Good, morality, rational self-control vs. freedom, complete control of environment (cf. Nietzsche, *Beyond Good and Evil*). Cultural significance of those ideals.
2. The methodological differences in Yoga, Shankara's Vedanta, Ramanuja's Vedanta; the relation between method and goal.
3. The nature of power acquired in Yoga and Vedanta.
4. The probable social behavior of a liberated man in terms of Yoga and Vedanta (cf. *Bhagavad Gītā*).

XIII. CLASSICAL INDIAN ART AND LITERATURE

A. Cultivation of aesthetic, as well as erotic, pleasure (kama) recognized as essential element of human life
   1. Literary works show importance of poetry, art, music, and dance in court and city life
   2. Brahmanic lawbooks stress moderation; pleasure secondary to concerns of religion and social responsibility (dharma)
   3. Texts on aesthetics develop refined theories of art
      a. Bharata's encyclopedic *Nāṭyaśāstra* (second century A.D.) analyzes and prescribes for every aspect of dramatic production
      b. Detailed manuals (shastras) of dancing, poetic composition, music

      c. Philosophers of art concentrate on the nature of aesthetic emotional experience (rasa)
         1) Creation and appreciation of rasa, first in dramatic productions, then in poetry; the poet, the poem or play, and the audience in relation to rasa
         2) Aesthetic bliss and final salvation (moksha); Abhinavagupta.
    4. Vaishnava theologians equate aesthetic relish (rasa) and religious devotion (bhakti)

B. Primarily religious function of public architecture and sculpture: objects of worship
    1. Buddhist relic mounds; Hindu temples
    2. Sculpture images as embodiments of gods; didactic reliefs, symbolic designs
    3. Canons of construction, proportion, iconography

C. Painting: few extant early works
    1. Wall painting: Ajanta Buddhist caves (Jataka themes), Sigiriya (Ceylon)
    2. Technical rules for fresco, color, modeling, etc.
    3. Miniature painting known only from medieval period

D. Drama: stylized spectacle
    1. Origins: Epic dialogues and episodes, popular farce, religious ceremony, dance
    2. Structure: aesthetic emotional atmosphere (rasa) depends on text and presentation
      a. Conflicts, plots, characters, poetry
      b. Mime, dance, music
    3. Characterization
      a. Stereotypes: royal hero, heroine, Brahman "fool"
      b. Languages vary with status: kings, Brahmans, courtesans speak Sanskrit; others speak different Prakrits (literary vernaculars)

E. Poetry
    1. Sanskrit kavya: elegant poetry composed to convey rasa
      a. Single lyric and gnomic verses known from collections; e.g. Bhartrihari
      b. Long lyrics: loosely-linked verses; e.g. Kalidasa, "Cloud Messenger"
      c. Court epics; based on *Rāmāyaṇa* literary forms; episodes of princely birth, battle, love, in series of elaborate stanzas; e.g. Kalidasa, "Birth of the War-God"
      d. Themes: love, seasonal beauty, war, court life, virtue and vice, worldly frustration

e. Condensed verse form: complex meters, elaborate rhetorical devices (e.g. pun, metaphor, synecdoche, irony), long compound words, alliterations, suggestive overtone (dhvani)

f. Interplay of human emotions and natural phenomena in the production of rasa

2. Classical Tamil poetry

a. Legendary academies (sangams); extant works ca. first to third centuries A.D.

b. Anthologies of short poems: love lyrics of "interior landscapes," court poems about kings, war, heroism, death

c. Collections of epigrammatic stanzas; e.g. Tiruvalluvar's *Kural*

d. Epic romances: dramatic narrative interspersed with lyric passages; depict aspects of Tamil civilization, e.g. *Silappadigāram* (The Ankle Bracelet)

e. Conventional imagery and structure infused with original details, dramatic situations, varied characters; idealized landscapes offset human situations

3. Prose narrative: literary forms in the story-teller tradition

a. Fable, e.g. *Pañcatantra:* animal characters; didactic verses as moral authority; concerns of everyday life

b. Romance, e.g. *Ten Princes:* picaresque themes, adventures in complicated society

Reading Assignment

Sources of Indian Tradition, 258–75; paperback, 256–70

Optional Assignments

Danielou, Alain. *Shilappadikaram (The Ankle Bracelet) By Prince Ilangô Adigal.* New York: New Directions paperback, 1965. A verse romance in Tamil; includes myth, history, custom, descriptions of city life, and interludes of lyric poetry.

Rowland, Benjamin. *The Ajanta Caves.* See IX above (review).

Ryder, Arthur (tr.). *Kalidasa: Shakuntala and Other Writings.* New York: Dutton paperback, 1959. The best available translation of this famous Sanskrit drama; also versions of Kalidasa's other works.

Additional Readings

Anthology of Indian Music, Volume One. World Pacific recording WDS-26200. Selections by musicians from the North and South Indian traditions, including Ravi Shankar, Ali Akbar Khan, Balachander. Sides five and six are a history and a short course in appreciation of Indian music, with examples, by Ravi Shankar. Accompanying notes.

Coomaraswamy, Ananda K. *The Transformation of Nature in Art.* Cambridge: Harvard University Press, 1934. Dover paperback, 1965. A comparison of theories of art in Indian, Chinese, and European medieval art, based on treatises of aesthetic theory, manuals, and literature.

De, Sushil Kumar. *Sanskrit Poetics as a Study of Aesthetic.* With notes by Edwin Gerow. Berkeley: University of California Press, 1963. A scholarly introduction to concepts and schools of poetic theory, addressed to the Western reader, while stressing internal developments.

Haas, George, C.O. (tr.). *The Daśarūpa: A Treatise on Hindu Dramaturgy by Dhanaṁjaya.* New York: Columbia University Press, 1912. "A treatise on the ten forms of drama" is drawn from the classical compendium of Hindu dramatic science, Bharata's *Nāṭyaśāstra.*

Ingalls, Daniel H.H. *Sanskrit Court Poetry from Vidyākara's "Treasury."* Cambridge: Harvard University Press, 1968. An abridged version of Ingalls' *Anthology of Sanskrit Court Poetry;* translated verses and notes are chosen for appreciation by a general audience.

Keith, Arthur Berriedale. *A History of Sanskrit Literature.* Oxford: Clarendon Press, 1928. Reprint 1953. *The Sanskrit Drama.* Oxford: Clarendon Press, 1924. Reprint 1959. The two volumes give a detailed survey of post-Vedic "classical" literature.

Kramrisch, Stella. *The Art of India.* London: Phaidon, 1954. A selective survey of Indian art, concentrating on classical sculpture and architecture; well illustrated, with introduction and notes.

Miller, Barbara Stoler (tr.). *Bhartrihari: Poems.* New York: Columbia University Press, 1967. A bilingual edition of Sanskrit poems attributed to Bhartrihari (ca. A.D. 400–450); lyric and epigrammatic verses expressive of life's conflicting concerns.

Ramanujan, A.K. (tr.). *The Interior Landscape: Love Poems from a Classical Tamil Anthology.* Bloomington: Indiana University Press, 1967. Extraordinary translations of spare, sensuous poems.

Renou, Louis. *Indian Literature.* Translated from the French *Les Littératures de L'Inde* (1951) by Patrick Evans. New York: Walker paperback, 1964. Brief introduction to works of major periods and literary languages.

Van Buitenen, J.A.B. (tr.). *Two Plays of Ancient India: The Little Clay Cart and The Minister's Seal.* New York: Columbia University Press, 1968. Translations which convey the stylized but lively character of the plays; informal Introduction on the Indian theater.

Zimmer, Heinrich R. *Myths and Symbols in Indian Art and Civilization.* Edited by Joseph Campbell. New York: Pantheon, 1946. Harper paperback, 1962. Impressionistic presentation of themes and motifs recurrent in Indian art and literature; plates.

For further bibliography and topics on drama, poetry, and fable see de Bary and Embree. *A Guide to Oriental Classics.* New York: Columbia University Press, 1964, 86–101.

Discussion Topics and Questions

1. Aesthetic values common to Indian painting, sculpture, poetry, music. How are elements used in each medium to create the aesthetic mood or atmosphere (rasa)?
2. The demanding role of the audience in classical Indian drama, poetry, music.
3. Compare the bases of unity in Indian drama with Aristotelian canons. What is the structural function of lyric poetry in Sanskrit drama and Tamil epic poetry?
4. Compare the stylization of characters in Sanskrit drama, Tamil epic, Greek tragedy. What do they reflect about cultural attitudes toward man's position in the scheme of things and towards the nature of "tragedy"?

XIV. TAMIL DOMINANCE IN SOUTH INDIA
(ca. 500–1300)

A. Isolation of the South prior to Muslim penetration
   1. Limited direct contact with northern states
   2. Peninsular rivalries
      a. Traditional territorial limits of southern coastal states; rival contemporary powers: Pandya, Chola, Chera, Pallava
      b. Conflict with successive dynasties of the western Deccan Plateau: Chalukyas of Badami, Rashtrakutas, Chalukyas of Kalyani, Yadavas, Holysalas
      c. Geographic basis: struggle for control of peninsular rivers
B. Sources
   1. Royal inscriptions, coin issues: chronology, political history
   2. Temple architecture, sculpture
   3. Tamil epics, Puram poetry

4. Chinese, Arab travelers' reports, e.g. Hsuan-tsang's visit to Kanchi (640) (cf. IX. C. 6.)
5. Ceylonese chronicles

C. Tamil kingdoms of Madras; extreme southern Pandya and Chera kingdoms subordinate
1. Pallava dynasty (height: mid-sixth to eighth centuries)
   a. Mystery of origin
   b. Extended power beyond traditional limits
   c. Narasimha-varman (ca. 625–645): outstanding ruler; founder of Mamallapuram, rock-hewn temples and reliefs
2. Chola dynasty (height: tenth to thirteenth centuries)
   a. Chronology known from accession of Pallava conqueror's son, Parantaka I (907): defeat of Pandya king, invasion of Ceylon
   b. Aggressive exploits of Rajaraja the Great and son Rajendra Choladeva I (ca. 985–1035): Deccan, East Coast to Bengal, Malabar Coast, Ceylon; naval power, annexation of offshore islands and expeditions to Southeast Asia
   c. Chola decline, reassertion of Pandya Kings in thirteenth century; Muslim inroads, Vijayanagar empire

D. Tamil administration
1. King: divine origin, hereditary succession; assisted by ministerial council, hierarchy of officials, subordinate princes
2. Village autonomy and internal organization: various village and district assemblies, local courts; continuity despite political changes at higher levels
3. Public works: temples, roads, dams

E. Maritime trade with Southeast Asia
1. Spread of Indian culture
2. Stimulation of merchantile activity

F. Tamil culture: Aryan-Dravidian synthesis
1. Influence of the Brahman minority: royal patronage for protectors of Vedic tradition; kings sought respectability through conformity to status tradition
   a. Sanskrit philosophy and literature
   b. Brahman social segregation; privilege based on religious knowledge and purity and economic power obtained through land grants and commerce; Brahman/non-Brahman dichotomy still characteristic of Tamil society
   c. Control of temple administration, education, ritual; stress on ritual purity, rigid caste regulations
2. Temple-centered Hinduism

54

    a. Social and economic focus of village, town

    b. Great temples under royal patronage, associated with court; retinue of temple attendants (Brahmans, devadasis or female slaves of the gods, servants), elaborate ceremonies, complex architectural projects

    c. Basis of formal education: Sanskrit models influence vernacular languages, literature

3. Continued activity and impact of Buddhist and Jain orders
4. Tamil devotional cults; theistic bhakti movements

    a. Sectarian hymns of Alvars and Nayanars

    b. Rejection of caste privilege, popular support, absorption of folk culture; simple ritual, popular language

    c. Modification of Brahmanic theology, e.g. Ramanuja's Vedanta; assimilation by orthodoxy, diffusion to North India

5. Tamil literature: influence of Sanskrit literary style, vocabulary; independent vigor of *Śilappadigāram,* Kamban's version of *Rāmāyaṇa*

Reading Assignments

Thapar, *History of India,* 167–220

Sources of Indian Tradition, 342–45, 353–57; paperback, 337–40, 348–52

Optional Assignment

Danielou, *Shilappadikaram.* See XIII above. Reread as sourcebook of Tamil culture.

Additional Readings

Majumdar, R.C. (ed.). *The History and Culture of the Indian People.* Volumes 3–5, *The Classical Age, The Age of Imperial Kanauj, The Struggle for Empire.* Bombay: Bharatiya Vidya Bhavan, 1954–1957. Chapters on dynasties of the Deccan and South India in these volumes cover the Gupta period to the time of the early Muslim invasion (ca. A.D. 500–1300).

Nilakanta Sastri, K.A. *A History of South India.* Second edition. London: Oxford University Press, 1958. The only scholarly survey of South Indian history. (For more detail, see the author's studies of the Chola and Pandya dynasties.)

Nilakanta Sastri, K.A. *Development of Religion in South India.* Bombay: Orient Longmans, 1963. Based on lectures delivered at the University of Chicago; deals with gods, religious sects, and philosophies of South India in historical context.

Rowland, Benjamin. *The Art and Architecture of India*. Baltimore: Penguin, 1953. Pp. 170–88, with plates, introduce aspects of South India architectuɾe and sculpture.

Discussion Topics and Questions

1. Geographic factors in Tamil history and culture.
2. The position of the South Indian vs. North Indian Brahman.
3. The economic significance of the political and religious institutions of rural South India.
4. Examples of architecture and sculpture as evidence of material and religious culture in South India; cf. *Śilappadigāram* descriptions.

XV. REGIONAL STATES OF NORTHERN INDIA
(ca. 650–1200)

A. Evolution of regional political pattern dated from death of Harsha (647): Indian medievalism
  1. Divisive struggles for control of Kanauj
     a. Gurjara-Pratihara domination (ca. 840–910)
     b. Pala dynasty of Bengal-Bihar; succeeded by Sena dynasty of Brahman origin (eleventh century)
     c. Rashtrakuta dynasty in the Deccan
  2. Emergence of numerous independent states
     a. Himalayan kingdoms: Nepal, Kashmir, Assam; relations with Tibet and China
     b. Kingdoms of northern and western plains: e.g. Chandelas, Paramaras (Raja Bhoja of Dhar: ideal Hindu prince) Solankis
     c. Small realms under self-declared kings (rajas) and great kings (maharajas)
B. Sources
  1. Inscriptions, copper land grant plates, coins
  2. Local "histories" and epics; e.g. Kalhana's chronicle of Kashmir, Rajasthani bardic narratives
  3. Arabic and Persian accounts
C. The Rajputs (Sanskrit: *rājaputra*, king's son)
  1. "Rajput" denotes tribe, clan, sept, or caste of warlike habits, making claim to aristocratic rank; treated by Brahmans as "Kshatriyas"

a. Sanskritization under Brahman tutelage
b. Creation of genealogies relating clans to solar/lunar races; respectability in Puranic tradition
2. No racial unity: diverse descent
a. Foreign invaders: upper ranks of invading Huns and accompanying tribes, e.g. Gurjaras; lower ranks became Hindu castes of lower status
b. Indigenous tribes, e.g. Chandelas of probable Gond origin
3. Assumption of ruler status by various clans in traditional republics of Rajasthan area; rise to political power ninth and tenth centuries
D. Indian "feudalism": basis of fragmentation and regional loyalty in political-economic structure
1. Ruler-vassal relationship
a. Kings grant land revenue to officers, selected holders ("vassals") in lieu of salary
1) Taxation of peasant cultivators
2) Theoretically only revenue rights granted; actually hereditary grants meant tenure and appropriation of land
b. Revenue used to pay king's share, levy armies (important as Turk, Afghan invasions increased)
c. Daughters in marriage to king
d. King's coinage used
e. Attendance at court on certain occasions
2. Decentralized administration
a. Vassals controlled groups of villages
b. Multiplication of sub-feudatories: diversion of income from cultivator and king by intermediaries
c. Surplus wealth drawn from land and village: subsistence farming
d. Lack of sufficient revenue at center: special taxes for public works, temples; further depression of peasantry
3. Aristocracy: narrow bases of political and economic power; dependence on land revenue; alienation from land
a. Military clans
b. Brahmans: granted land in return for status services
c. Mutual protection of privilege: social stagnation
E. Cultural life: efflorescence of local traditions
1. Regional and local dynastic histories
2. Vernacular as well as Sanskrit literature encouraged
3. Courts vied for craftsmen to build monumental temples, e.g. Khajuraho, Bhubaneshwar

F. Raids of Mahmud of Ghazni (1000–1025)
   1. Loose organization of Hindu rulers
   2. Temple pillage; Somnath expedition
   3. Alberuni's survey of Hindu culture
G. Muslim invasions under Muhammad of Ghor (1191–1205): establishment of Muslim power in India
   1. Prithviraja
      a. Led resistance to Muhammad; captured (1192)
      b. Popular hero of northern India; celebrated in vernacular epics and bards' songs
   2. Plunder of Banaras; defeat of Raja Jaichand (1194)

Reading Assignment

Thapar, *History of India,* 221–65

Additional Readings

Alberuni. *Alberuni's India.* Translated by E.C. Sachau. Two volumes. London: Trubner, 1888. Reprint, Delhi: S. Chand and Co., 1964. Abridged edition by Ainslie T. Embree, New York: Norton paperback, 1971. The account of the Muslim historian who spent several years in India in the service of Mahmud of Ghazni; information on the culture of North India in the eleventh century.

Kalhana. *Rājataraṅgiṇī.* Translated by M.A. Stein. (London, 1900) Reprints, Delhi: R.S. Pandit, 1967; London: S. Probsthain, 1935. A chronicle of the Kashmir kings, written in the twelfth century; one of the rare history texts in Sanskrit.

Majumdar, K.C. (ed.) *The History and Culture of the Indian People.* Volumes 3–5, *The Classical Age, The Age of Imperial Kanauj, The Struggle for Empire.* Bombay: Bharatiya Vidya Bhavan, 1954–1957. Chapters on the dynasties of North Indian in these volumes cover the period from the fall of Harsha to the time of the early Muslim invasions (ca. 647–1300).

Tod, James. *Annals and Antiquities of Rajasthan.* Two volumes. Revised edition. London: Routledge and Kegan Paul, 1957–1960. Originally published in 1829; an account of the Rajput states based on literary sources and traditions. Daniel Thorner's "Feudalism in India" in *Feudalism in History* (Princeton: Princeton University Press, 1956) examines Tod's use of the concept of "feudalism."

Rowland, Benjamin. *The Art and Architecture of India.* Baltimore:

Penguin, 1953. Pp. 153–70, with plates, introduce the architecture and sculpture of Medieval North India.

Discussion Topics and Questions

1. Compare Indian "feudalism" with feudal systems commonly known from Europe; especially nature of the economic contracts involved.
2. The relationship between Brahmans and Rajputs in Medieval India.
3. The economic, social, and religious significance of monumental medieval architecture in North India.
4. Indian vulnerability to Muslim raids and invasions.

XVI. DEVOTIONAL HINDUISM

A. Bhakti ("devotion")
   1. Personal relationship between worshipper and supreme deity; love, reciprocity
   2. Sectarian theism: devotion to Vishnu (Rama or Krishna incarnations), Shiva, Devi (the Goddess)
B. Complex background
   1. *Bhagavad Gītā:* bhaktiyoga (discipline of devotion); Krishna as the Lord (Bhagavan); cf. VIII. F. 4
   2. Epic and Puranic mythology
      a. Incarnations of sectarian gods: anthropomorphic personalities and exploits
      b. Popularity of *Rāmāyaṇa* and *Bhāgavata Purāṇa:* the characters of Rama and Krishna
   3. Puranic ritual: vows, pilgrimage, offerings
   4. Popular and esoteric cults
   5. Systematic philosophy: elaborate doctrines adapted to bhakti, especially Vedanta mysticism; cf. XII
   6. Aesthetics: aesthetic emotion (rasa); cf. XIII. A. 3–4
   7. Erotic poetry: theme of parted lovers; cf. XIII. E
   8. Islamic mysticism: Sufi teachings and practice
C. Devotion in poetry
   1. Hymns of Tamil "saints"; Shaiva Nayanars, Vaishnava Alvars: grace, submission (seventh to ninth centuries)
   2. Jayadeva's *Gita Govinda:* Sanskrit lyric drama (twelfth century)

    a. Krishna's spring rites among the cowgirls; the estrange-
       ment and reunion of Krishna and Radha

    b. Sensuous and erotic context of songs and descriptions

    c. Allegory of soul's longing for God (?)

  3. Kirtans (song offerings) of Mirabai: Rajasthani princess, searching for vision of Krishna (sixteenth century)

  4. Bengali Vaishnava lyrics: laments of Krishna's mistresses (sixteenth to seventeenth centuries)

  5. Hindi *Rāmāyaṇa* of Tulsidas (1532–1623): emphasis on orthodox forms of love; Rama as faithful husband, loving king, worshipped brother

  6. Examples in every regional language

D. Practice of devotion

  1. Puja (worship); songs of devotion, music, dancing; offerings of flowers, incense, colored powders to images

    a. Image as representation of deity, aid to focusing devotion

    b. Temple as abode of God; service to God

    c. Household shrine; daily rites

  2. Ancestral rites

  3. Seasonal festivals, e.g. Holi in spring

  4. Pilgrimages to cult centers, e.g. Puri in Orissa (Car Festival); Madura in Madras

  5. Tantric cults: ritualization of practices forbidden by Hindu dharma; e.g. magical diagrams, incantations (mantras), sexual rites

Reading Assignments

Thapar, *History of India,* 256–65
Sources of Indian Tradition, 327–66, 411–24; paperback, 322–61, 410–17

Optional Assignments

Beals, Alan. *Gopalpur.* See X above. Pp. 54–57.
Dimock, Edward C., Jr., and Denise Levertov. *In Praise of Krishna: Songs from the Bengali.* Garden City, New York: Doubleday, Anchor paperback, 1967. Translations of Vaishnava love lyrics.
Lewis, Oscar. *Village Life in Northern India.* See X above. Pp. 197–246.

Additional Readings

Archer, W.B. *The Loves of Krishna in Indian Painting and Poetry.* London: Allen and Unwin, 1957. New York: Grove Press paperback, 1960. A survey of religious texts, poetry, and painting relating to various aspects of the Krishna theme.

Bharati, Agehananda. *The Tantric Tradition*. London: Rider, 1965. An analysis by an Austrian-born anthropologist and Tantric initiate of the intellectual and ritual contents of Hindu and Buddhist Tantrism, elements of which appear in popular and esotic cults of Hinduism.

Bhattacharya, Deben. *Love Songs of Chandidās, The Rebel Poet-Priest of Bengal*. London: Allen and Unwin, 1967. New York: Grove Press paperback, 1970. *Love Songs of Vidyāpati*. London: Allen and Unwin, 1963. New York: Grove Press paperback, 1970. *Songs of the Bards of Bengal*. (First published as *The Mirror of the Sky*.) London: Allen and Unwin, 1969. New York: Grove Press paperback, 1969. Readable translations, with introduction and notes, of the poems of two medieval devotional poets and a contemporary group of wandering bards.

Brown, W. Norman. "Mythology of India," in S.N. Kramer (ed.), *Mythology of the Ancient World*. See II above; parts 3–6 (289–314) discuss aspects of the sectarian gods Vishnu and Shiva and the Mother Goddess.

Brown, W. Norman (ed. and tr.) *The Saundaryalaharī or Flood of Beauty*. Harvard Oriental Series, volume 43. Cambridge: Harvard University Press, 1958. A widely used devotional poem addressed to Devi, the Goddess; it belongs to early Tantric Hindu Shaktism. Sanskrit text, translation, and photographs of an illustrated manuscript.

Dimock, Edward, C., Jr. *The Place of the Hidden Moon: Erotic Mysticism in the Vaiṣṇava-Sahajiyā Cult of Bengal*. Chicago: University of Chicago Press, 1966. A study of the sixteenth century antinomian cult which attempted to unite eroticism and religion; provides a scholarly but readable introduction to the complex phenomenon of cult origin, literature, and practice, which is basic to Hinduism.

Hein, Norwin. "The Rām Līlā," in Milton Singer (ed.), *Traditional India: Structure and Change*. Philadelphia: American Folklore Society, 1959, 73–98. A description of the dramatic presentation of the *Rāmāyaṇa* episodes of Sita's abduction and recovery, as performed in religious festivals of North India.

Singer, Milton. *Krishna: Myths, Rites, and Attitudes*. Honolulu: East-West Center Press, 1966. Chicago: University of Chicago paperback, 1969. Articles discussing various aspects of Krishna worship.

Discussion Topics and Questions

1. Antecedents of medieval devotionalism in Indian religious and literary traditions; examples.
2. The relationship of devotion (bhakti) between the God and his devotee: the effect of love suffered in separation.
3. Resolution of the conflict between passion (kama) and religious duty (dharma) through devotion (bhakti).
4. Social significance of personal worship (puja) and vernacular languages in devotional cults vs. sacrifice (yajna) and Sanskrit in Brahmanic religion.

XVII. ISLAM AND MUSLIM CULTURE

A. Origin of Islam
   1. Arabian peninsula; Middle East
   2. Blend of tribal cultures minimizing individual freedom, emphasizing public law
   3. Significant role of Quraish tribe, recently settled in Mecca, commercially strong
   4. Muhammad (b. Mecca, ca. 570–580), member of respectable Quraish family
      a. Revelations begin at age 40; thinks of himself as prophet
      b. Opposition in Mecca
      c. Flight or Hegira to Medina ca. 622; leader of community there
      d. Muslim calendar dates from Hegira
      e. Thought based on Arabian traditions, own inspiration, contact with Judaism and Christianity
      f. Search for purer monotheism: distinctive teachings, institutions
   5. Basic teachings
      a. *Koran:* basic text of 114 chapters accepted as directly inspired word of God told through his prophet; highest authority and basis for later legal and philosophical developments in Islam
      b. Sunna: body of custom and practice based on Muhammad's words and deeds; next most important basis of Islamic law and thought
         1) Corpus of canonical tradition about Prophet (*Hadīth*)

2) Chain of sources for each statement (hadith) established to weed out forgeries
   c. *Shari'a:* law of Islam based on *Koran* and Sunna; disagreements in interpretations settled by concensus of the community (ijma)
   d. Concept of Islamic community (umma): tie of common faith has precedence over all other ties; based on pre-Islamic Arabian community of blood ties
      1) Religious and political community
      2) Practices which bind community together, e.g., fasting, daily prayers, almsgiving, pilgrimage to Mecca
      3) Injunction to fight in the way of God against nonbelievers (jihad)
B. Rapid spread of Islam
   1. Striking phenomenon of history: wave of conquest across Middle East, North Africa, to India within century of Muhammad's death
   2. Forced conversion of conquered peoples to Islam, with exceptions
      a. "People of the book": religion based on a holy book
      b. Hindus classified as people of the book: legal position conforms to reality of a subject population too large to kill or convert
   3. Non-Arab participation in ruling process; incorporation of non-Arab customs
   4. Arab Abbasid Caliphate in decline by ninth century; local Muslim dynasties founded
   5. Establishment of Samanid dynasty in northeastern Persia by Islamicized, landed Persian aristocracy (ca. 892)
   6. Separation of Ghaznavid, nomadic Turks, from Samanid state during tenth century; carry Islamic and pre-Islamic Persian practices into India
      a. Concept of transferable iqta (revenue collection unit) for nobles
      b. Idea of kingship
   7. Arab conquest of Sind (712); raids in north India in following centuries; greater Muslim contact through traders and missionary groups
C. Religious and political developments
   1. Sunnis: followers of the Sunna, majority of Muslims
      a. Recognize regular succession to the Caliphate and concept of concensus of community

b. Political dominance through most of Islamic world
   c. Religion of the Turkic conquerors of India
2. Shi'as: the other principal group of Muslims
   a. Origin in political movement among Arabs who supported Ali (Muhammad's son-in-law) and descendants as true Caliphs
   b. Non-Islamic practices and beliefs, e.g., glorification of leader (imam) as absolute authority
   c. Official religion in Persia (ca. A.D. 1500); significant role in Indian history during Mughal period
3. Sufism
   a. Roots in popular religion emphasizing mysticism and personal relationship between man and God
   b. Fraternities of ascetics
   c. Growth despite opposition from orthodoxy
   d. Well-organized orders, recognized saints, large popular following by eleventh century
4. Al-Ghazali (d. 1111): compromise between orthodox Islam and Sufism
   a. Impersonality of orthodox Islamic thought
   b. Key to faith in Sufi experience of personal God
   c. Respectability of Sufism within Islam

Reading Assignment

Sources of Indian Tradition, 367–435; paperback, 362–428

Optional Assignments

Gibb, H.A.R. *Mohammedanism.* New York: Oxford University paperback, 1962, chapters 1–8. The best short introduction to Islam.
Ikram, S.M. and Ainslie T. Embree. *Muslim Civilization in India.* New York: Columbia University Press, 1964. A general survey of the period of Muslim supremacy in India.

Additional Readings

Arberry, A.J. *Sufism.* London: Allen and Unwin, 1956. A short but excellent exposition of the development and ideology of Sufism.
Lewis, Bernard. *The Arabs in History.* New York: Harper & Row, 1960. An excellent account of the early years of Islamic development which sets Islam within a cultural and social framework.
Nicholson, R.A. *The Mystics of Islam.* Chester Springs, Pennsylvania: Dufour, 1962. A more poetic account than Arberry's, which gives a good idea of the more personal feelings involved in Sufi thought.

Titus, Murray T. *Islam in India and Pakistan*. Calcutta: Y.M.C.A. Publishing House, 1959. A comprehensive account of the development of the Islamic community in India from a cultural point of view.

Von Grunebaum, Gustav. *Medieval Islam*. Chicago: University of Chicago paperback, 1969. Useful introduction to the development of Islamic thought and institutions.

Discussion Topics and Questions

1. Analyze the career of Muhammad and the impact of his teaching on the peoples of Arabia.
2. What factors aided the spread of Islam? How was the situation changed after the decline of the Arabs as a political force?
3. What significance was there in the development of Sufism? Can Sufism be compared with any movements within religious traditions other than Islam?
4. Is it significant that certain groups of Muslims, rather than others, carried Islam to north India?

XVIII. THE DELHI SULTANATE

A. Sources include Persian histories and chronicles
B. Invasion of Turkic Muslims in Northwest India from Central Asia (ca. 800–1200)
    1. Initial quest: money and slaves
    2. Establishment of bases in India
    3. Technological and tactical superiority over most Indian foes, e.g., better iron swords and stirrups, better horses; better discipline in moving large armies; experience in bureaucratic organization of large territory
    4. Raids by Mahmud of Ghazna (ca. 1000–1025), to acquire wealth for financing wars
    5. Conquest of northern India by Ghuride successors to Ghaznavids (ca. 1175–1200)
C. Muslim penetration of India
    1. Sultanate period defined in terms of political domination by successive Turkic dynasties
    2. Important social and economic developments associated with beginning date
        a. Growth of cities in Northern India in thirteenth century
        b. Increase in commerce in thirteenth century

    c. Development of centralized bureaucracy which partially suppressed former feudal structures

D. Turkic dynasties (ca. 1206–1526)
1. Ghurides (1206–1290): control exercised by small number of noble families supporting oligarchy
2. Khaljis (1290–1320): "new men" who begin opening army bureaucracy to men of lower (usually Muslim) origins
3. Under Alauddin Khalji (1296–1316) sultanate reaches highest degrees of centralization and greater control over nobles
4. Tughluqs (1320–1398): strive for greater centralization; nobility's protest leads to relaxation after 1350
5. Timur's invasion (1398)
6. Sayyids and Lodis (1414–1526): Sultanate fragmented; Sultan first among equals; political fragmentation accompanied by decline in trade and urban life

E. Administration and economy
1. Administration and land revenue collection
    a. Tradition of centralized rule, inefficient in practice
    b. Rule in many places through Hindu chiefs who collect revenues from peasants
    c. In theory government right to fixed percentage of peasants' produce
    d. Beginning of long-term conversion of independent rulers into landlords
    e. Iqta system: bureaucratic land grants to important nobles who were officials or army officers
2. Economic and social development
    a. Extension of cultivation, e.g., Bengal
    b. New craft production in cities to support Sultanate establishment, e.g., weaving, metal work, paper
    c. Integration of tribal groups in caste structure
    d. Growing disparity between ritual and economic position of craftsmen

F. Spread of Islam
1. Theologians and scholars (ulama) flee before Mongol invaders of Middle East and enter India, spurring development of intellectual community
2. Mystical sects effect more conversions than theologians
    a. Chishti and Suhrawardi orders
    b. Centers of learning and spiritual guidance
    c. Adoption of Hindu customs in heavily Hindu areas
3. Conversions to Islam among lower castes and non-Hindus

     a. By Sufis, not military men
     b. Urban concentration: craftsmen (e.g., weavers) working for Muslim rulers
     c. Rural converts: e.g. East Bengal, lower peasants less assimilated to Hinduism
G. Hindus under the Sultanate
   1. Few forcible conversions
   2. Some major Hindu rulers incorporated into revenue systems as landlords
   3. Peasants little affected: taxes increased, more security than under warring Hindu rulers

Reading Assignment

Thapar, *History of India,* 266–336

Optional Assignment

Ikram, S.M., and Ainslie T. Embree. *Muslim Civilization in India.* See XVII above. Chapters III–VIII.

Additional Readings

Elliott, H.M., and John Dowson. *The History of India as told by its own Historians.* Eight volumes. Allahabad: Kitab Mahal, 1964. Reprint. The largest collection of translations of Persian histories of India. Invaluable for the Sultanate and Mughal periods, even though the translations are not of complete works and are sometimes inaccurate.

Habib, Mohammad, and Afsar Umar Salin Khan. *The Political Theory of the Delhi Sultanate.* Allahabad: Kitab Mahal, 1961. Translation of a work by the most important political theorist of the Sultanate period (Ziauddin Barani). Provides considerable insight into the issues and modes of thinking of the times.

Habibullah, A.B.M. *The Foundation of Muslim Rule in India.* Revised edition. Allahabad: Central Book Depot, 1961. The best work on the early period of Muslim rule; combines solid research with judicious interpretation.

Lal, K.S. *History of the Khaljis, A.D. 1290–1320.* Revised edition. New York: Asia Publishing House, 1967. Chapters on economic policy and administration of this standard work are particularly interesting and provide material for a comparison with the policies of the next centralizing emperor, Akbar.

Moreland, W.H. *The Agrarian System of Moslem India.* Cambridge: Heffer, 1929. Although somewhat dated, still contains the best economic interpretation of the Sultanate period to be found in one volume.

Nizami, K.A. *Some Aspects of Religion and Politics in India during the Thirteenth Century*. Bombay: Asia Publishing House, 1961. A clear and useful study which offers some new interpretations as well as new information (particularly on religion); shows continuities with and shifts from earlier Islamic and Indian practices.

Discussion Topics and Questions

1. Why were the Turks successful in conquering and ruling large areas of northern India?
2. To what extent did the introduction of Muslim rule effect the economy, technology, and social organization of northern India?
3. What happened to the political leaders of Hindu society after the conquest?
4. How was Muslim religious life organized in northern India?

XIX. THE MUGHALS

A. Historical sources
  1. Persian histories
  2. Fuller land revenue and administrative records than previously in Indian history
B. Turkic people from inner Asia, speaking Chaghatai, a Turkic language; Sunni Muslims; claim of descent from great Central Asian conquerors, Timur or Tamerlane (the Turk) and Ghengis Khan (the Mongol); latter claim basis of misnomer "Mughal"
  1. Most important Muslim dynasty: long-lasting accomplishments in administration, arts, culture
     a. Stable bureaucracy and military establishment; groundwork for British Raj
     b. Increased trade and urbanization
  2. Rulers: Babur (1526–1530 in India); Humayun (1530–1556), in exile (1540–1555) while Sher Shah and successors ruled in North India; Akbar (1556–1605); Jahangir (1605–1627); Shah Jahan (1628–1658); Aurangzeb (1658–1707)
C. Society and economy
  1. Ruling group: emperor, his family, leaders of bureaucracy, military, a few religious leaders

a. Almost all mansabdars (see below, D. 2)

b. Leadership in hands of 500–700 people

2. Role of the Hindu zamindars (landholders serving as revenue collectors)

a. Rulers work through them using force and rewards

b. Mughal policy alternates between strengthening Muslim mansabdars and strengthening zamindars

3. Peasants

a. Variation in social organization

b. Rich collectively dominate villagers; kinship group

c. Poorer lower castes often excluded from landholding

4. Trade and industry

a. Few technological innovations

b. Increase in external and internal trade; but high costs make transport of bulk goods uneconomic and production is increasingly localized (e.g., cotton)

c. Sophisticated networks of banking and trading houses

1) Seths have houses Agra, Banaras, Dacca

2) Interest rates compare favorably with European

3) Large sums can be transferred by check

D. Mughal administration

1. Emperor

a. Theory: Abul Fazl, Akbar's chronicler, extends Muslim-Persian conception of Emperor exalted far above subjects

b. Functions

1) Theoretic control over all appointments, promotions, military decisions

2) Despotic power curtailed by practical difficulties

3) Appointments made in Emperor's name by high officials

4) Bribery and favoritism

2. Mansabdari system

a. Military ranking system established by Akbar

b. Means of rewarding civilian and military officials

c. Ranks expressed in terms of horsemen to be provided and bureaucratic position

d. Mansabdars dominate administration

1) Mainly Muslims, some from outside India with strong ties to places of origin

2) Transfer of posts about every four to five years

3) Control through efficient record system

4) Ideally capable of any job, in practice many specialized (e.g., in revenue department)

5) Land grants or jagirs in lieu of salary

69

3. Jagir lands
   a. Temporary revenue rights given to mansabdars
   b. Transfer to avoid establishment of territorial bases
   c. Most empire land in jagirs: substantial revenue outside imperial treasury
4. Administrative decisions and levels
   a. Empire divided into provinces (12 at beginning of Akbar's reign, 21 under Aurangzeb)
   b. Several administrative subdivisions in each province
   c. Officials appointed at all territorial levels: revenue collectors, maintainers of control
5. Subordinate states
   a. Concentration of large states in Rajasthan and border areas
   b. Semi-independent, paying tribute to center, retaining own revenue collections
   c. Important cultural traditions
   d. Potential focal points for rebellion

E. Decline of the Mughals
1. Civil resistance and rebellion
   a. Increase in last third of the seventeenth century: growing pressure on revenue system made by Aurangzeb's Deccan wars
   b. Major cause: peasant unrest, sometimes with zamindari leadership; revenue farming by absentee mansabdars; administrative control increasingly arbitrary
2. Aurangzeb and the decline
   a. Rigidity of his personality
   b. Alienation of Hindu groups, despite increase of Hindu mansabdars
   c. Campaigns in south drain financial and psychological resources of empire; increased pressure on revenue system
     1) Conquests of Bijapur and Golconda: creation of new mansabdars
     2) Insufficient jagir land: mansabdars begin to favor looser system

Reading Assignments

Spear, *History of India,* 15–60
Sources of Indian Tradition, 436–508; paperback, 429–500

Optional Assignment

Ikram, S.M., and Ainslie T. Embree. *Muslim Civilization in India.* See XVII above. Pp. 133–253.

Additional Readings

Athar Ali, M. *The Mughal Nobility under Aurangzeb.* Bombay, New York: published for the Department of History, Aligarh Muslim University by Asia Publishing House, 1966. An important and largely statistical study of the composition of Aurangzeb's mansabdars which suggests possibilities for many new interpretations of political history.

Bernier, François. *Travels in the Moghul Empire.* Revised edition. Translated by A. Constable; edited by V.A. Smith. London: Oxford University Press, 1934. Insightful descriptions of Mughal court life and rule by a French physician who resided at Aurangzeb's court from 1658–1670.

Chandra, Satish. *Parties and Politics at the Mughal Court, 1700–40.* Aligarh: Aligarh Muslim University, Department of History Publications no. 15, 1959. Very good study of Mughal court during the period of decline. Also contains his theory of the crisis of the jagirdari system which led to the Mughal decline.

Elliott, H.M., and John Dowson. *The History of India as told by its own Historians.* See XVIII above.

Fazl, Abul. *Ain-i-Akbari.* Translated by H. Blochmann and H. Jarrett; revised translation of volume II by J. Sarkar. Calcutta: Royal Asiatic Society of Bengal, 1948–1949. The most important administrative work from the Mughal period. Provides insight into the problems of ruling, the nature of society, and Mughal organization of administration.

Habib, Irfan. *The Agrarian System of Mughal India (1556–1707).* Bombay: Asia Publishing House, 1963. A basic and important work on the economic history of the Mughals and of India generally.

Qureshi, I.H. *The Administration of the Mughal Empire.* Karachi: University of Karachi, 1966. Best study of Mughal administration; can also serve as an introduction to what might be termed the "Pakistani view" of Mughal history.

Tripathi, R.P. *Rise and Fall of the Mughal Empire.* Allahabad: Central Book Depot, 1956. A useful political account covering the period from the early sixteenth century to the end of the Shah Jahan's reign.

Discussion Topics and Questions

1. What did it take to become a successful imperial ruler in premodern India? Compare the efforts of Akbar and of Alauddin Khalji.

2. Describe the operation of the mansabdari and jagirdari systems. How significant were they as a means of controlling the nobility?
3. It has been said that the Mughals were the first Muslims to attempt to be rulers of all the people of northern India. Is this statement true? How successful do you think they were?
4. What was the place of the zamindars within Indian society during Mughal times?
5. What factors were most significant in the decline of Mughal power?

XX. CULTURAL AND RELIGIOUS LIFE, SIXTEENTH TO EIGHTEENTH CENTURIES

A. Reform movements affecting religious thought and organization within Hinduism and Islam; widespread syncretism (fifteenth to sixteenth centuries)
   1. Hindu religious reformers in Bengal, North India, Maharashtra, e.g., Chaitanya (b. 1485), Nanak (b. 1469)
      a. Devotional religion emphasizing man's individual and emotional ties to God
      b. Differences between Hinduism and Islam minimized; focus on inner self
   2. Modified Sufism; accepted within Islamic establishment
   3. Popular devotional monotheism of Kabir (b. 1440)
B. Islamic establishment under Mughals: from liberal experimentation under Akbar to conservative rigidity under Aurangzeb
   1. Akbar: attracted to mystical-devotional practices and beliefs
      a. Investigation of Islamic religious heritage (1560s)
      b. Goal of reforming Islam (1570s)
      c. Opposition of orthodox ulama
      d. Investigation of other religions (Hinduism, Jainism, Christianity) 1578–1579
      e. Small circle of followers, mostly Muslims, regarding him as religious leader
      f. His faith called Din-i-Ilahi (Divine Faith)
      g. Personal vision and withdrawal from leadership of Islamic community
   2. After Akbar: Islamic establishment more conservative
   3. Shah Jahan: some temple destruction, dislike of high-ranking Hindus

4. Aurangzeb
   a. Dislike for Hinduism and unorthodox Muslim practices
   b. Champion of orthodox Islam from 1670s
   c. Temple destruction and reimposition of tax for non-Muslims (jizya)
5. Dara Shikoh, Aurangzeb's brother: interest in similarity between Islamic and Hindu mysticism
6. Orthodox Islam more conservative in 1700 than in 1550; continued Hindu-Muslim mingling on village level
C. Islamic cultural and religious influence
   1. Persian-Islamic influence in Mughal period
      a. Persian used as language of administration from thirteenth century
      b. Continuous emigration from Iran and Afghanistan; strengthened ties to Persian culture
   2. Urdu
      a. Language of the army camp and bazaar
      b. Literary language by eighteenth century, replacing Persian as cultural language in North India; signifies Indianization of upper-class Muslims
   3. Mughal patronage of the arts
      a. Poets and artists from Middle East and various parts of India
      b. Mughal miniature painting under Akbar and Jahangir
      c. Aurangzeb's disapproval of most artistic expression and decline of patronage
   4. Architecture: impressive structures of high quality
      a. Fatehpur Sikri, capital built by Akbar
      b. Taj Mahal and other buildings in Agra: pinnacle of Persian culture in India
      c. Jami Masjid and Red Fort in Delhi: expressive of Indo-Islamic culture
D. Hindu-Muslim interaction
   1. Greater at high political levels during sixteenth to early seventeenth centuries than later
   2. One-nation and two-nation theories of later leaders of India and Pakistan read back into this period
E. Rise of the Sikhs
   1. Distinctive set of customs and beliefs drawn mainly from Hinduism, little substance from Islam; strong influence of medieval bhakti figures
      a. Hindu bhakti figures, e.g., Ramananda (1425–1475):

stress on personal God and use of vernacular language
  b. Muslim bhakti figures, e.g., Kabir: possibility of all seeking and finding God
  2. Sikh founder: Guru Nanak (1469–1538)
    a. "Sikh" derived from Sanskrit term for pupil; guru mediates between man and God
    b. Nanak from dominant caste in Punjab; became beggar, then preacher
    c. Stressed love of one formless God and joyful submission to Him
    d. Criticized Hindu idol worship and caste inequities; in tradition of Hindu reforming sects
  3. Line of Sikh gurus associated with transformation from religious group into highly organized community and small state
    a. Angad (1539–1552): distinctive script and free kitchen for Sikhs
    b. Amar Das (1552–1574): separation of Sikhs from asceticism, caste, Brahman dominance
    c. Arjun (1581–1606): circles of Sikhs and *Ādi Granth* (First Book) compilation of Sikh sayings; in local script
      1) Guru is like God
      2) Sikhs better organized, clash with Mughals
    d. Hargobind (1606–1645): military leader as well as guru
    e. Guru Gobind Singh (1675–1708): militant community of Sikhs (khalsa)
      1) Mechanisms for dealing with stress: local councils of five
      2) Five K's: uncut hair, comb, bangle, dagger, short pants
      3) Local Gurdwaras like temples
      4) Recruitment among untouchables as well as caste Hindus
      5) Gobind Singh succeeded by the Khalsa rather than an individual
  5. Some Sikh orders separate in following period; reform movements into twentieth century

Reading Assignment

Sources of Indian Tradition, 509–18, 531–49; paperback, 501–10

Optional Assignment

Welch, Stuart Cary, and Milo Cleveland Beach. *Gods, Thrones, and Peacocks. Northern Indian Painting From Two Traditions: Fifteenth to Nineteenth Centuries.* New York: Asia Society paperback, 1965. Insights into Indo-Muslim culture through Rajput and Mughal painting; well illustrated.

Additional Readings

Ahmad, Aziz. *Studies in Islamic Culture in the Indian Environment.* Oxford: Oxford University Press, 1964. A scholarly interpretation of Islamic cultural and intellectual history.

McLeod, W.H. *Guru Nanak and the Sikh Religion.* Oxford: Oxford University Press, 1968. A scholarly and interesting interpretation of the nature and history of Sikh religion.

Qureshi, I.H. *The Muslim Community of the Indo-Pakistan Subcontinent.* The Hague: Mouton, 1962. A useful study of Indian Muslims from the time of the conquest, which gives a good deal of cultural material and presents the Pakistani point of view.

Rizvi, Athar Abbas. *Muslim Revivalist Movements of the 15th and 16th Centuries.* Agra: Agra University, 1965. Excellent study of important religious developments of the period.

Russell, Ralph, and Khurshidul Islam. *Three Mughal Poets.* Cambridge: Harvard University Press, 1968. An interesting view of Islamic cultural development in India, and of the interaction between Muslim and non-Muslim culture.

Sharma, S.R., *Religious Policy of the Mughal Emperors.* Second edition. Bombay: Asia Publishing House, 1962. Standard work, detailing shifts in religious policy and attempting to interpret the personal religious views of the emperors.

Singh, Khushwant. *The Sikhs.* London: Allen and Unwin, 1953. Best short account of the Sikhs.

Wellesz, Emmy. *Akbar's Religious Thought Reflected in Moghul Painting.* London: Allen and Unwin, 1952. An interesting and useful attempt to explore the ideas of a man and his culture through the evidence of paintings.

Discussion Topics and Questions

1. Discuss the Muslim contributions to high culture in India.
2. To what extent was Islamic culture in India affected by the Indian cultural and intellectual environment?
3. What similarities are there, if any, between Sufism and the bhakti movements?
4. Was there one culture or two or many in Mughal India?
5. What role did political considerations play in the religious views and activities of the Mughal emperors?

Modern India

BOOKS FOR ASSIGNED READINGS

General Readings on Modern India

Brecher, Michael. *Nehru. A Political Biography*. London: Oxford University Press, 1959. This wide-ranging, well-written biography deals with all the major areas that Jawaharlal Nehru touched upon and thus may serve as a general text for the period 1920–1959. The paperback edition is too brief to be of value.

Brown, W. Norman. *The United States and India and Pakistan*. Revised edition. Cambridge: Harvard University Press, 1963. A brief and intelligent account of the development of India and Pakistan, utilizing a thematic approach.

Chaudhuri, Nirad C. *The Autobiography of an Unknown Indian*. New York: Macmillan, 1951. University of California paperback, 1968. A sensitive and insightful account of an Indian intellectual from East Bengal, describing his own life and cultural and political currents that shaped him. The author also gives a fascinating picture of Calcutta and of Hindu-Muslim relations.

de Bary, Wm. Theodore (ed.). *Sources of Indian Tradition*. New York: Columbia University Press, 1958. Paperback (in two volumes), 1964. The second part of this work (paperback volume II) presents selections from many important modern Indians and a few significant documents of the British Raj.

Thompson, Edward, and G.T. Garratt. *Rise and Fulfilment of British Rule in India*. Reprint. Allahabad: Central Book Depot, 1962. Original edition, 1934. Although an older work, this text is extremely well written, judicious in its judgments of the British and the Indians, and, on balance, still serves as one of the best introductions to the period.

Woodruff, Philip. *The Men Who Ruled India*. Volume I, *The Founders*. Volume II, *The Guardians*. London: Jonathan Cape,

1953, 1954. Schocken paperback, 1964. Written by a former civil servant and deals with the British who served in India, their careers and their outlook. This work reads easily and gives a fine feeling for the men who manned the British Raj.

Other Recommended General Readings

Marx, Karl. *On Colonialism and Modernization.* Edited by Shlomo Avineri. Garden City, New York: Anchor paperback, 1969. This collection includes Marx's important writings about India, the most suggestive of which is "The British Rule in India."

Metcalf, Thomas. *Modern India—An Interpretive Anthology.* London: Collier-Macmillan, 1971. A valuable collection of essays analyzing themes in nineteenth- and twentieth-century Indian history.

Moore, Barrington, Jr., *Social Origins of Dictatorship and Democracy. Lord and Peasant in the Making of the Modern World.* Boston: Beacon Press, 1966 and paperback. A stimulating comparative study of the routes six countries, including India, have taken towards or into the modern world. The author stresses the sociological factors that have impeded India's progress in modernizing.

McLane, John R. (ed.). *The Political Awakening in India.* Englewood Cliffs, New Jersey: Prentice Hall, Spectrum paperback, 1970. A useful collection of documents with brief, informative introductions by the editor.

Majumdar, R.C., H.C. Raychaudhuri, and Kalikinkar Datta. *An Advanced History of India.* London: Macmillan, 1960. Paperback, 1969. A text that covers the whole sweep of Indian history; it covers cultural as well as political developments and has a nationalist bias.

Philips, C.H., H.L. Singh, and B.N. Pandey. (eds.). *The Evolution of India and Pakistan 1858 to 1947, Select Documents.* London: Oxford University Press, 1962. An extensive and extremely useful collection of source materials drawing on British and Indian records, private correspondence, and resolutions of political organizations.

Philips, C.H. (ed.). *Historians of India, Pakistan and Ceylon.* London: Oxford University Press, 1961. Interesting and informative essays on historical writing and historical consciousness in South Asia. The work is divided into three parts: Ideas of History in the Early Empires and Literatures; India in the period of Muslim Rule; Historical writings in the Periods of European Dominance and the Nationalist Movements.

Sayeed, Khalid B. *Pakistan, The Formative Phase 1857–1948*. Second edition. London: Oxford University Press, 1968. The most useful general account of the developments of Muslim political consciousness and separatism.

Smith, Vincent A. *The Oxford History of India*. Third edition edited by Percival Spear. Oxford: Claredon Press, 1958. Spear has rewritten the modern section, more detailed than his other texts for the modern period; this text has a British bias and is written in the tradition of British histories of India, but may serve as useful reference work.

Spear, Percival. *A History of India*. Volume 2. Baltimore: Penguin, Pelican paperback, 1965. Spear has written three accounts of the modern period, from this most cursory one to a very detailed version (on the nineteenth century) in the *Oxford History of India*. Although none is very satisfactory, one of them may be substituted for Thompson and Garratt.

Spear, Percival. *India. A Modern History*. Ann Arbor: University of Michigan Press, 1961. This text covers all of Indian history, but is more detailed for the modern period. Spear has a British bias and insufficient sensitivity to Indian nationalism. He deals more interestingly with the period of his service in India in the two decades before independence.

I. EUROPEAN EXPANSION AND INDIA ON THE EVE OF EUROPEAN CONTACT

A. India at the time of Europe's Renaissance expansionism
1. Mughal decline
    a. Overextension of empire into Deccan and South India
    b. Contradictory aims of participants in agrarian system
    c. Internal revolts by Sikhs, Marathas, Jat rebels near Agra, and, in 1672, Satnamis
    d. As consequence of Aurangzeb's bigotry Shi'a and Hindu allies lost
    e. Further hypothesis: decline in quality of elite
2. Successor states in eighteenth century
    a. Not clear in mid-century which power will win out
    b. Marathas (including Scindia, Gaekwar, Holkar, Bhonsla of Berar) strong in west and raid across country
    c. Sikhs strong in northwest during later eighteenth to early nineteenth century
    d. Other regional powers include Hyderabad, Oudh, Bengal
    e. Europeans, particularly British and French, becoming important militarily
3. Continuities and changes flow from Mughal and earlier times into age of European domination
B. Stages of European intrusion
1. One set of waves in time of late Renaissance, commercial revolution
    a. In wake of Marco Polo (thirteenth century) Portuguese, Dutch, later French, British explorers and traders to the East
    b. Technological advances, especially in navigational techniques
2. Traders from the sea
    a. Enter on the periphery of Mughal empire
    b. Go to interior seeking trading concessions
    c. Trade in spices, silks, saltpeter, indigo, cotton goods

C. The European companies
  1. Portuguese: Crown control
     a. Trading factories along coast of Africa, Asia in sixteenth century
     b. Goa, capital, held from 1510 until after Indian independence in 1961.
     c. Limited territorial ambitions
     d. Lose monopoly of oceanic routes in seventeenth century
  2. Dutch: Netherlands East India Company founded 1602
     a. Seventeenth to early eighteenth centuries: established many trading bases in India, including Calicut, Cochin, Negapatam, several in Bengal
     b. Company overseas headquarters in Batavia
     c. Trading profits fade in eighteenth century and government takes over company's possessions
  3. English: East India Company; chartered 1599 with limited subscriptions; 1614 joint stock company
     a. Bases for trade established in India: 1612 Surat; 1646 Fort St. George, Madras; 1665 Bombay; 1690 Calcutta, Fort William
     b. Middle class, merchants fighting for markets
     c. 1698 crisis; two companies; 1709 fusion with New Company
     d. By 1717, three fortified areas in Madras, Bombay, Calcutta regions; web of territorial responsibilities and trading connections
     e. Company servants do both Company work and private trade
     f. By 1730, Company prepared military forces to defend its bases
     g. Until 1773 no close government check; Company loans to government to maintain monopolies
  4. French: Compagnie des Indes; founded by Colbert 1664
     a. Many Indian trading bases on Carnatic, in Bengal, on Malabar Coast; capital at Pondicherry
     b. Peak in 1740s; then backing and profits fail
  5. French and English companies become contestants for power by mid-eighteenth century
     a. French led by Dupleix late 1740s to 1753
     b. He builds subsidiary alliances; uses Indian rulers
     c. Dupleix recalled 1753
     d. French and English fight 1756 to 1763 on several continents

      e. English win and gain supremacy among Europeans in India

D. Theories of European imperialism to be tested on Indian case
  1. Parker Moon, *Imperialism and World Politics,* 1926
     a. "Aggressive men if not aggressive nations"
     b. Beginning of worldwide diplomacy, interconnections
  2. Hobson, *Imperialism,* 1902
     a. Differentiates imperialism from colonialism; former has large native population, latter settlements of colonials predominate
     b. "Small minority wielding political or economic sway over a majority of alien and subject people . . ."
  3. Lenin, *Imperialism,* 1917
     a. Monopolies of finance capital play decisive role in economic life and must export capital
     b. International capitalist monopolies complete territorial division of world among themselves
     c. Lenin's theory tied to specific historical moment
  4. Joseph Schumpeter, "The Sociology of Imperialism," in *Imperialism and Social Classes,* 1919
     a. Atavistic remnants, earlier aristocratic dreams of war and glory, hang on into modern, rational, capitalist times
     b. Rational capitalism itself does not generate drive for empire, war instincts, or ideas of overlordship
  5. These studies overestimate control of home powers and profits of empire; do generate questions for analysis

Reading Assignments

Brown, *United States and India and Pakistan,* chapters 1, 2
Sources of Indian Tradition, 553–65; paperback, 3–13
Thompson and Garratt, *Rise and Fulfilment of British Rule,* book I
Woodruff, *Men Who Ruled India,* volume I, part I

Optional Assignments

Cohn, Bernard S. "Political Systems in Eighteenth Century India: the Banaras Region," *Journal of the American Oriental Society,* 82, no. 3 (1962), 312–19. A skillful analysis and answer to those who have viewed eighteenth-century India as the scene of unmitigated anarchy.

Schumpeter, Joseph. *Imperialism and Social Classes.* New York: Meridian, 1955. One of the most stimulating essays on the phenomenon of imperialism.

Additional Readings

Carrington, C.E. *The British Overseas*. Second edition. Cambridge: Cambridge University paperback, 1968. A useful general survey of the development of the British empire in different parts of the world.

Edwardes, S.M., and H.L.O. Garrett. *Mughal Rule in India*. Delhi: S. Chand, 1962. A succinct outline of Mughal history and suggestions about the decline of the Mughal dynasty.

Fieldhouse, D.K. *The Colonial Empires*. New York: Delacorte Press, 1967. A general history of all the major European empires stressing the eighteenth and nineteenth centuries.

Furber, Holden. *John Company at Work*. Cambridge: Harvard University Press, 1951. A thorough study of the European companies in India, their trade and politics in the late eighteenth century.

Parry, J.H. *Europe and a Wider World 1415–1715*. London: Hutchinson's, 1949. A short, standard account of the beginnings of European expansion.

Discussion Topics and Questions

1. Should European expansion before the mid-nineteenth century be called "imperialism"?
2. What are the most convincing explanations of the Mughal decline?
3. Was European rule in India "inevitable"?
4. Assess the argument that the Europeans came to South Asia at a time of anarchy and they, particularly the British, wrought order out of chaos.

II. BRITISH TRIUMPH AND PROBLEMS OF EMPIRE

A. East India Company victorious in struggle between successor states
   1. Numerous arguments offered by European and Indian historians in nineteenth to twentieth centuries to explain British triumph
      a. Evolutionary necessity: British best at struggle for survival (Sir Alfred Lyall)
      b. Theological necessity: European Christians must convert Hindu heathens and Muslim infidels

c. Political and character theories (Sir Jadunath Sarkar; I.H. Qureshi)
   1) Indian weakness of leadership offers opening to Europeans
   2) British superior at civil and military organization and in quality of leadership (Sir Percival Spear)
d. Accident theory: British stumbled into an empire (H.H. Dodwell)

2. How the British conquered
   a. Important role of military leader Robert Clive (1725–1774)
      1) Fights French in south and uses native rulers; 1751 victory at Arcot
      2) Victory over Bengali Nawab Siraj-ud-Daulah at Plassey, 1757, and installation of Mir Jafar as nawab
      3) Clive and other top officials take huge rewards
      4) Clive as Governor of Bengal; returns to England 1760–1765
      5) Again Governor of Bengal and Commander-in-Chief, 1765–1767
   b. Using Company and royal troops and alliances with native rulers, conquerors move inward from coastal bases
      1) Rationale of more defensible borders often given, e.g., for Warren Hastings' Rohilla campaign, 1774
      2) Wellesley's eagerness for empire (Governor-General 1798–1805): to reach stability must take more and more
      3) Accessions and conquests: Bengal, 1765; Banaras, 1775; Mysore, 1799; Hyderabad, 1800; Tanjore and Surat, 1801; Peshwa, 1802; Maratha territories, 1817–1819; Sind, 1843; Sikh territories, 1846–1848; Satara, 1848; Jhansi, 1853; Nagpur, 1854

B. Problems of empire
1. Question of legitimacy and changing objectives of British: by end of early nineteenth century accept that they have an empire and want subjects' loyalty.
2. How the system works and areas of strain
   a. Organization of the Company in London
      1) Court of Directors: from 1709 there are 24 with considerable patronage; co-chairmen called "Chairs"
      2) Court of Proprietors or the General Court of Stockholders
      3) Ties to city financial interests
      4) Company group in parliament

5) In eighteenth century Company goes into debt for administration and war
b. Gradual shift from Company to Crown: delimitation of Company by acts of Parliament
   1) North's Regulating Act, 1773
      a) Governor-General and Council established in India, but former's power limited
      b) Supreme Court to try Europeans' cases
      c) Attempt to limit private trade
   2) Pitt's India Act, 1784
      a) More power to Governor-General in council and over other presidencies (those besides Bengal, i.e., Bombay and Madras) after Warren Hastings hampered by limited powers of office
      b) Board of Control set up between Parliament and Company
      c) Henry Dundas as President of Board, 1784–1801, shapes its powers
c. Warren Hastings (1732–1818)
   1) From clerk to Council member to Governor to first Governor-General (in 1774)
   2) Ends Clive's system of dual or indirect rule in many areas
   3) Insists on responsibility in administration
   4) Tries to systematize courts
   5) Land revenue collection experiments not successful
   6) Sympathy for Indian culture
   7) Conflict with Philip Francis in his council
   8) Later tried on charges of misdeeds in India
d. Cornwallis, Governor-General and Commander-in-Chief, 1786–1793
   1) Development of central secretariat with general, revenue, and trade boards
   2) Civil service established with better salaries and no private trade
   3) Permanent Settlement of Bengal (see IV below)
e. Regional and district administration
   1) Governors in Madras and Bombay
   2) In districts, judge-collector office
      a) Use of Indians for most lower jobs in administration
      b) Head of district travels around to oversee
f. Strains between man-on-the-spot and men at home

1) Communications between London and India take two years (round-trip) criticism at home of expansionism in India
2) Strains between presidencies and Calcutta
3) Strains between district heads and regional headquarters
g. 1813 Act of parliament at time of company charter renewal
1) End of company monopoly on India trade
2) Company forced to admit principle of missionary activity

Reading Assignments

Thompson and Garratt, *Rise and Fulfilment of British Rule,* books II, III
Woodruff, *Men Who Ruled India,* volume I, part II

Optional Assignments

Frykenberg, Robert Eric. *Guntur District 1788–1848.* Oxford: Clarendon Press, 1965. A pioneering district history which shows in penetrating fashion how British rule impinged on a local area—how the British used the Indians and how the Indians often used the British.

Marshall, P.J. *Problems of Empire: Britain and India 1757–1813.* London: Allen and Unwin, 1968 and paperback. A useful collection of documents with a lengthy, insightful introduction.

Additional Readings

Embree, Ainslie T. *Charles Grant and British Rule in India.* New York: Columbia University Press, 1962. Through the skillful and incisive examination of the career of an important Company official, the author explores the nature of British rule in the late eighteenth and early nineteenth centuries.

Feiling, Keith. *Warren Hastings.* London: Macmillan, 1955. A useful though occasionally confusing biography of a crucial figure in the development of the Raj.

Macaulay, Lord (Thomas). "Lord Clive" and "Warren Hastings" in *Critical, Historical, and Miscellaneous Essays.* Six volumes. Boston: Houghton Mifflin, 1860. Brilliantly written, extremely opinionated, seminal essays on the two crucial figures in early Company rule.

Philips, C.H. *The East India Company 1784–1834.* Manchester: Manchester University Press, 1940. Reprint, 1961. A standard and thorough work on the Company at its height and in decline.

Discussion Topics and Questions

1. What was the importance of India in British life in the eighteenth and early nineteenth centuries?
2. What was the significance of the British in Indian life in the middle of the eighteenth century? At the end of the eighteenth century?
3. Discuss the problem of the differential impact of the British on India.
4. Evaluate the theories and rationales given for British expansion in India by the protagonists and by later writers.

III. THE MEN WHO RULED INDIA AND WESTERN ATTITUDES TOWARD INDIA

A. The British in India
  1. Is it possible to talk about British "national character"? Are there common features in the personalities of many who go to India?
     a. Some suggestions: adventureousness; seriousness; hardness in times of stress; belief that they were unique in commercial enterprises; awareness of class distinctions without being bound by them; pride of country
     b. Habit of authority: its exercise and acceptance
  2. What groups supply recruits?
     a. Scots in Company, administration, business
     b. Irish in army
     c. Nineteenth century: London, Company, and rural gentry families
     d. Shift through nineteenth century to more clerical and professional backgrounds for I.C.S.; more open recruitment
B. Eighteenth-century life of British in India
  1. Informality; mixing with Indians more easily than later
  2. "Nabob": tales of great fortunes
     a. Many died in India, up to two-thirds
     b. Very few made great fortunes
C. Creation of Civil Service
  1. Cornwallis instrumental in cutting private trade, increasing salaries
  2. Indians pushed out of responsible positions

3. Self-image of the unselfish, intelligent, British (Platonic) guardian of India
4. Model for British civil service
D. Training and acculturation
   1. Fort William College, Calcutta
      a. Founded by Wellesley in 1800
      b. Controversy over college intertwined with other issues
      c. Declines after 1814; language training continued to 1854
      d. Vernacular or regional languages taught
      e. Orientalist attitudes conveyed to young civilians
      f. Research in India culture and ties to Asiatic Society of Bengal
   2. Haileybury, near London
      a. Founded in 1805 to train Company servants
      b. Takes over much of Fort William's work
      c. Languages, political economy, Indian subjects taught
      d. "Old school" ties formed by its graduates: learn to flaunt authority together and not to "sneak"
      e. About 87 percent pass final examinations
      f. Possibly evangelical and utilitarian influences conveyed
      g. Closes in 1857
   3. Competitive examination system from late 1850s
      a. Civil Service opened to all who do best in mental and physical exam
      b. Trickle of Indians into service in later nineteenth century
   4. Socialization of civil servants
      a. Rise in class by going to India
      b. Make connections in school, on boat to India, and through letters of introduction
      c. After initial language training, look down on Indians; may think of only as scheming, unfit people on basis of court and revenue experience
      d. Responsibility at early age; quickly think they know all; learn to fit Sahib role
   5. Civil service only about 5 percent of total Europeans in services
      a. Others include forestry, police, artisans, businessmen, women, missionaries
      b. About 500,000 British in India by end of nineteenth century
   6. Strains in British Indian society
      a. Divisions between officials and nonofficials

91

      b. Vigorous settlement life from late eighteenth century: little Englands in India

      c. European women come in greater numbers in nineteenth century

      d. Women help to separate British social life from Indian society

    7. Commitment to India

      a. Some nonofficials (as well as officials) make India their calling

      b. A variety of motivations and range of callings

      c. Some examples:

         1) Social service: Verrier Elwin, Mother Theresa

         2) Cultural and religious involvement: Sister Nivedita, Christopher Isherwood, Annie Besant

         3) Workers for Indian nationalism: Nivedita, Besant, C.F. Andrews

         4) Workers for world revolution or communism in India: Philip Spratt in 1920s

         5) Scholarship and literary work: Edward Thompson, William Jones

E. Western attitudes towards India: shape expectations and experiences of those who go

    1. Ancient and medieval views:

      a. Vast, flat, marvellously wealthy land

      b. Land of despotism and miracles

    2. French seventeenth-century travelers and eighteenth-century philosophers

      a. Continuity with ancient views in Montesquieu

      b. Voltaire: civilization's childhood in East; lessons for West, but now static

    3. British: two main currents and many mixtures

      a. Sympathetic, orientalizing strain (Orientalists, romantics, Theosophists; Isherwood; other believers in sterility of West)

      b. Critical, hostile, modernizing strain (Grant, Macaulay; missionaries; utilitarians)

    4. Orientalists: late eighteenth and nineteenth century

      a. William Jones and others build idea of Indian golden age

      b. Long period of decline with little creativity

      c. Modern revival possible under British rule and tutelage

    5. Utilitarians (Bentinck as Governor-General; James and John Stuart Mill in India Office)

a. Want to improve India from above
  b. Severe criticism of uncivilized India and rapacious Brahmans in James Mill's *History of British India*
  c. Blends with other paternalistic strains in nineteenth century
6. Changes over time in British attitudes
  a. Nineteenth century imperial confidence and belief that British can improve India
  b. In time of rising Indian nationalism, doubt and melancholy

Reading Assignments

Sources of Indian Tradition, 587–601; paperback, 35–49

Thompson and Garratt, *Rise and Fulfillment of British Rule,* book IV, chapter II

Woodruff, *Men Who Ruled India,* volume I, part III, chapters I-XI

Optional Assignments

Forster, E.M. *A Passage to India.* New York: Harcourt, Brace, 1924. The most famous novel written by an Englishman about the British Raj in India. On the surface a tale of the involvements of British and Indians and the near impossibility of real friendship and communication between them. On a subtler level it touches on existential problems of all human creatures, symbolized abstractly by arches, echoes, and silence and concretely by the mosque, caves, and the temple.

Mannoni, O. *Prospero and Caliban, The Psychology of Colonization.* Second edition. New York: Praeger paperback, 1962. A fascinating exploration of the relationship between the rulers and the ruled in colonial areas. The author draws on literature, psychoanalysis, existentialism, and his practical experience as an administrator in Madagascar in formulating his ideas.

Stokes, Eric. *The English Utilitarians and India.* Oxford: Clarendon Press, 1959. A masterful analysis of the impact of utilitarianism on British policy and administration in India in the nineteenth century.

Additional Readings

Bearce, George D. *British Attitudes towards India 1784–1858.* London: Oxford University Press, 1961. Although the author's categories of "conservative," "humanitarian," and "liberal" often overlap, his survey of attitudes in this period is very useful as a starting point for a more exacting inquiry.

Carstairs, Robert. *Human Nature in Rural India*. London: William Blackwood, 1895. Interesting reflections and analyses by a Bengal civilian who lived for many years in rural India. His writing reveals a good deal about British attitudes towards Indians and British self-imagery.

Greenberger, Allen J. *The British Image of India*. London: Oxford University Press. 1969. A useful survey of British novels set in India, 1880–1960. The major themes traced are the British self-image, the Indian scene, and Anglo-Indian relations; the author sees a movement from imperial confidence to doubt and finally to melancholy.

Ingham, Kenneth. *Reformers in India 1793–1833*. Cambridge: Cambridge University Press, 1956. Valuable study of missionaries' work vis-à-vis caste, idolatory, sati, education, the status of women, and the transmission of Christianity to India.

Lach, Donald F. *Asia in the Making of Europe*. Volume I. Chicago: University of Chicago Press, 1965. A panoramic survey of European interaction with Asians from ancient times.

Notestein, Wallace. *The English People on the Eve of Colonization 1603–1630*. New York: Harper Torchbooks, 1962. Sensitive and interesting analysis of English character and society in the seventeenth century.

Seeley, J.R. *The Expansion of England*. London: Macmillan, 1883. An important argument for the imperial connection which reveals various attitudes towards India and the mother country in the later nineteenth century.

Spear, Percival. *The Nabobs*. London: Oxford University Press paperback, 1963. A stimulating survey of English social life in India during the eighteenth century.

Thornton, A.P. *The Imperial Idea and its Enemies*. London: Macmillan, 1959. An important study of proponents and opponents of imperialism in the late nineteenth century.

Yule, Henry, and A.C. Burnell. *Hobson-Jobson*. New edition edited by William Crooke. Delhi: Munshiram Manoharlal, 1968. Reprint of 1903 edition. A fascinating glossary of British Indian terms and vocabulary which gives the flavor of the British Raj.

Discussion Topics and Questions

1. In what ways is it useful to talk about British or Indian national character? In what ways misleading?

2. Are there several patterns of British acculturation in India or one dominating pattern?
3. What consistency has there been over the centuries in Western attitudes towards India? When do new themes enter: what are they?
4. What were some of the regional and communal stereotypes that the British had of the Indians? How did these shape British rule? How did they change over time?
5. How accurate was the Indian civil servant's image of himself as a Platonic guardian?

IV. ECONOMIC AND SOCIAL DEVELOPMENTS UNDER COMPANY RULE

A. Economic changes: on the land
    1. India peasant, agricultural society; changes in landholding patterns, land taxes vital concern to many
    2. British responsible from late eighteenth century for tax collection over increasing area
        a. Investigation of and changes in land revenue settlements
        b. Colonial problem: with whom do you make settlements?
        c. Combination of British experience, economic ideas, and conceptions of Indian situation
        d. Usually unforeseen consequences
    3. Permanent Settlement in Bengal
        a. Experiments with different systems 1750s to 1790s
        b. Under Cornwallis settlement *in perpetuum* at fixed rate
        c. Settlement with mixed group called zamindars
            1) Includes various types of holders and taxpayers
            2) Difficulties in homologizing zamindars
            3) Actual peasant cultivators not adequately safeguarded
        d. Consequences
            1) Great number of land transfers and fall of some great landholders
            2) Growth of rentier strata; i.e., numerous intermediate holders during nineteenth century
    4. Settlements in United Provinces
        a. Banaras region permanent settlement like Bengal
            1) Rajputs become permanent tenants, controlling two-thirds of land

2) Peasant cultivators at bottom of social structure as before
     b. Mahalwari settlement: attempts to settle with corporate landholding lineage groups
  5. Madras: zamindari as well as ryotwari settlements
     a. Ryotwari: settlements by "ryots," or those who manage peasant cultivators
     b. Ending of slavery and growth of percentage of landless laborers
  6. Bombay Presidency: area around Poona
     a. Tenuous balance between rights of corporate groups and cultivators lacking guaranteed tenancy
     b. Attempt at settlement with rich peasants
     c. Dominant, wealthier peasants benefit; temporary migration of some cultivators
  7. Comparisons of the different settlements in late nineteenth century
     a. In most areas (except Oudh, Punjab) 30–40 percent of land held by big landholders
     b. 60–70 percent held by very large number of petty landholders
     c. Rich get richer regardless of settlement
B. Economic changes: patterns of trade
  1. Seventeenth to eighteenth centuries: internal trade vital; foreign trade not a large part of economy
     a. Finished silks, cotton goods, spices to Europe
     b. Bullion imported into India until European dominance
  2. Nineteenth-century changes
     a. Overall expansion of trade, especially overseas trade
     b. India becomes exporter of raw materials, importer of certain manufactured goods
        1) Raw cotton exports grow
        2) Imports of finished cotton goods increase rapidly
        3) Some argue that market enlarged and that shift does not show destruction of Indian textile industry
  3. India pays certain costs of empire
     a. "Home charges" for Indian administration
     b. Additional charges for defense of empire outside India
     c. India finances Britain's deficit; Hobsbawm estimates two-fifths before World War I
  4. Shift in concentration from commerce to growing British capital investment

a. British investors help build Indian railroads and make handsome profit

b. Laissez-faire does not apply to India

C. Urbanization and de-urbanization under Raj

1. Decline of some cities that flourished under Mughals; e.g., Murshidabad, Dacca in Bengal

2. Rise of new imperial cities

a. Center on seacoast that connect world outside India with interior; e.g., Bombay, Madras, Calcutta

b. Administrative, economic, cultural functions of these cities

c. Both Europeans and Indians identify with them

d. Trading groups, literati, wealthier drawn to them

e. Disproportionately Hindu; also Marwaris, Parsis, foreign trading groups

3. Revival and growth of some older urban centers; e.g., Delhi, Ahmadabad

D. Problem of the "new middle classes" (also see XII below)

1. Analysis of urban phenomena

a. Description usually of professional, not entrepreneurial middle class; a social category, no apparent class consciousness

b. Changes in occupational structure; legal, medical, administrative, teaching positions open up; small, but rising percentage of Indian civil servants

c. Upper and lower classes not specified

2. Rise of powerful, wealthy families under Raj

a. Serve Raj and derive advantages

b. Examples: Debs and Tagores in Calcutta

Reading Assignments

Brown, *United States and India and Pakistan,* chapter 3

Thompson and Garratt, *Rise and Fulfilment of British Rule,* book IV; book V, chapters I–IV

Optional Assignments

Frykenberg, Robert E. (ed.). *Land Control and Social Structure in Indian History.* Madison: University of Wisconsin Press, 1969. A recent and extremely stimulating collection of articles which stresses regional and district studies dealing with the nineteenth century in India.

Misra, B.B. *The Indian Middle Classes.* London: Oxford University Press, 1961. A compendium of some useful data on the growth of what the author calls the commercial, industrial, landed, and educated middle class, particularly in the nineteenth century. The work is marred by a lack of conceptual sophistication in approaching the question of class.

Additional Readings

Cotton, H.E.A. *Calcutta Old and New*. Calcutta: W. Newman, 1907. An old but interesting history of Calcutta which reveals the great attachment some Europeans had to the "Second City of the Empire" at the height of the British Raj.

Davis, Kingsley. *The Population of India and Pakistan*. Princeton: Princeton University Press, 1951. A succinct analysis of the growth and changes in the Indian population since the late nineteenth century, using the Indian census which began in 1872. There are brief and useful chapters on urbanization as well.

Frykenberg, Robert E. *Guntur District, 1788–1848*. Oxford: Oxford University Press, 1965. See II above.

Guha, Ranajit. *A Rule of Property for Bengal*. Paris: Mouton, 1963. An elegantly written account of the intellectual background of the idea of a Permanent Settlement of the land revenue in Bengal.

Hobsbawm, E.J. *Industry and Empire. An Economic History of Britain since 1750*. London: Weidenfeld and Nicolson, 1968. Penguin paperback. A brilliant general economic and social history which analyzes, *inter alia,* the connections between the British and Indian economies.

Kumar, Dharma. *Land and Caste in South India*. Cambridge: Cambridge University Press, 1965. A pioneering study, using some statistical methods, which focuses on the problem of the relative number of landless laborers in Madras during the nineteenth century.

Kumar, Ravinder. *Western India in the Nineteenth Century*. London: Routledge and Kegan Paul, 1968. A useful regional study dealing with the economy, politics, and society of Bombay from 1818 to 1918.

Mukherjee, Nilmani. *The Ryotwari System in Madras*. Calcutta: Firma K.L. Mukhopadhyay, 1962. A standard work on the formulation and implementation of the land revenue settlement in Madras in the nineteenth century.

Discussion Topics and Questions

1. Compare the making of the land revenue settlements in different

parts of India during the nineteenth century. What were the consequences of the various settlements?

2. Analyze the evidence for and against the "drain" on the Indian economy in the nineteenth century.

3. Who were the "new middle classes"? In what ways did they constitute a middle class? In what ways did they not?

4. Describe the processes of urbanization at work in nineteenth century India. What is meant by "urbanization"?

V. EDUCATIONAL AND CULTURAL CHANGES IN NINETEENTH-CENTURY INDIA

A. Education
  1. Traditional Indian education
     a. Small number of pupils surrounding Hindu or Muslim teacher
     b. Teaching often by rote
     c. In cultural centers and rural areas
  2. Beginnings of Western education
     a. Impetus from well-to-do Indians who see economic advantages
     b. Also support from missionaries and other Europeans
     c. Becomes crucial ingredient for social mobility
     d. Schools, then colleges in Presidency towns
     e. Spread in nineteenth century to other cities and rural areas
  3. Government role
     a. Concern among Orientalists for Indian culture, languages
     b. 1813 charter renewal; provision for small allotments for traditional Hindu and Muslim learning
     c. Macaulay's Minute on Education, 1835
        1) Declares value of Indian learning, culture to be dubious
        2) Presses for Western education, English language as medium at higher levels
        3) Western subjects in Indian colleges
     d. Wood Despatch, 1854
        1) Concern for lower level of education and vernacular medium of instruction
        2) Inadequately implemented
     e. Three affiliating universities on British model, 1857
        1) Calcutta, Madras, Bombay universities set examinations

2) Students attend classes in affiliated colleges
3) Numbers of students:

Entrance exams, 1857–1880	No. of candidates	No. passed	%
Calcutta	17,588	8,327	47
Bombay	6,747	1,145	17
Madras	4,562	1,227	27

   4) By early 1880s: 100 arts and professional colleges with 9,000 students; 456 secondary schools with 60,000 students
  4. Muslims lag in Western education, especially areas where they are majority
  5. Question of medium of instruction unsettled
     a. Indian regional languages neglected
     b. Language issue later intertwined with nationalism
B. Problems of Westernization and cultural change
  1. Many possible units to be investigated: country, region, city, village, social group, family, individual, literary genres, painting
  2. Indian cultural traditions living into nineteenth century
     a. Lyric poetry and longer narrative poetic forms
     b. Learned texts and commentaries
     c. Cultural-religious practices
        1) Religious cults
        2) Folk plays
     d. Regional languages as rich and flexible vehicles with untold possibilities
  3. Influence of Western education and culture
     a. Changes in life style; e.g., living and eating habits, dress, entertainment, patterns of expenditure
     b. On regional languages
        1) Development of prose writing and Western punctuation adapted to Indian languages
        2) New media of communication adapted from West (e.g., newspapers)
     c. Some consider ferment a renaissance, e.g., Bengal Renaissance in the nineteenth century
        1) Cultural forms adopted from West (e.g., novels, essays, press) but build also on Indian genres
        2) Creativity not on such a level that it can be called "renaissance" by European standards

d. Development of associational life crucial for nationalism; e.g., Young Bengal in 1830s espousing extreme Westernism

e. New jobs and professions with models in West and ancient India; e.g., doctors, lawyers, teachers

f. Influence of Western religion
  1) Missionaries gain converts to Catholicism and Protestantism
  2) Converts in urban centers and tribal areas
  3) Missionaries also active in education, medicine, language work

g. Social reform activity, stimulated by Indian reformers, government, missionaries
  1) First half of nineteenth century government measures against sati, female infanticide backed by Indian reformers
  2) Second half of nineteenth century government passive; must be pushed by Indian reformers to act
  3) Reformers work for marriage reform, emancipation of women
      a) Ishwar Chandra Vidyasagar (1820–1891), Vishnu Shastri Pundit (1827–1876), Behramji Malibari (1853–1912), D.K. Karve (1858–1962), Jotiba Govind Phule (1827–1890) working in Bengal and Bombay for widow remarriage, raising marriage age, female rights and education
      b) Hindu Widows' Remarriage Act XV, 1856; Native Marriage Act III of 1872; and Age of Consent Act, 1891, passed after reformers' campaigns but ineffectively implemented
  4) Some reformers criticize Brahmans' narrowing often destructive role in Indian society; e.g., Gopal Hari Deshmukh (1823–1892), Gopal Ganesh Agarkar (1857–1895), Keshub Sen, and Dayananda Saraswati (see VI below)
  5) Social reformers' papers include Malibari's *Indian Spectator* and *East and West;* K. Natarjan's *Indian Social Reformer*
  6) National Social Conference begins 1887, linked to annual Congress sessions; M.G. Ranade (1842–1901) most instrumental in it
  7) Phule and others turn more to work for untouchables; concern for their plight grows in twentieth century

Reading Assignments

Sources of Indian Tradition, 565–601; paperback, 13–49

Thompson and Garratt, *Rise and Fulfilment of British Rule,* book IV, chapter IV

Optional Assignments

McCully, Bruce T. *English Education and the Origins of Indian Nationalism.* New York: Columbia University Press, 1940. A thorough study of the growth of Western education in India in the nineteenth century and of the spread of Western political ideas as a consequence of this education.

Srinivas, M.N. *Social Change in Modern India.* Berkeley: University of California Press, 1966 (also in paperback). An attempt at analyzing the long-term processes of Sanskritization and Westernization by a prominent anthropologist.

Additional Readings

Adam, William. *Reports on the State of Education in Bengal (1835 and 1838).* Edited by Anathnath Basu. Calcutta: University of Calcutta, 1941. A fascinating survey by a government officer of the educational institutions in the villages of rural Bengal and Bihar.

Bose, Nirmal Kumar. *Modern Bengal.* Calcutta: Vidyodaya Library, 1959. A preliminary and suggestive study of change in a town, a family, and a caste.

Coleman, James (ed.). *Education and Political Development.* Princeton: Princeton University Press, 1965. A wide-ranging collection of essays, of value in placing Indian developments in comparative perspective.

De, Sushil Kumar. *Bengali Literature in the Nineteenth Century.* Calcutta: Firma K.L. Mukhopadhyay, 1962. A masterful study of continuities with the past, innovations and changes in Bengali literature by a famous Sanskritist.

Heimsath, Charles H. *Indian Nationalism and Hindu Social Reform.* Princeton: Princeton University Press, 1964. A valuable general study of social reform movements in Bengal, Bombay, Madras, and North India; concentration on the later nineteenth century and on the interrelationship of nationalism and social reform.

Kopf, David. *Orientalism and the Origins of the Bengal Renaissance.* Berkeley: University of California Press, 1969. A detailed study containing useful information about important cultural and educational institutions shaped by European Orientalists, missionaries, and Bengalis in the early nineteenth century.

McDonald, Ellen E., "English Education and Social Reform in Late Nineteenth Century Bombay: A Case Study in the Transmission of a Cultural Ideal," *Journal of Asian Studies*, XXV, no. 3 (May, 1966), 453–70. An interesting study suggesting that certain Western social ideals were transmitted to the students of Bombay and thus helped to shape the social reform movements in that area.

Tandon, Prakash. *Punjabi Century*. New York: Harcourt, Brace and World, 1961 and paperback. An autobiographical account which illuminates the interaction between Western and Indian cultures in the period 1857 to 1947.

Discussion Topics and Questions

1. What continuities and discontinuities were there between traditional Indian education and the educational institutions and practices developed in nineteenth-century India?
2. How might we define "Westernization"? "Modernization"?
3. What influences has Western education had on Indian cultural and religious traditions?
4. Why was the growth of Western education uneven in the different regions of India, and what have been some of the consequences of that unevenness?

VI. NINETEENTH-CENTURY CULTURAL MOVEMENTS

A. General character
   1. Draw syncretically upon a variety of Indian traditions
   2. Draw as well on Western traditions
   3. Select, amalgamate, change materials drawn upon
   4. General aim: to find purified Indian truth
      a. Compatible with Indian traditions
      b. Critical of present conditions
B. Brahmo Samaj
   1. Grows from Brahmo Sabha founded by Rammohun Roy (1772–1832)
      a. Gathers a group around himself in Calcutta from 1817
      b. Advocates purified, monotheistic Hinduism

c. Claims this is original form of the religion
   d. Supports Western education, freedom of press, abolition of sati
2. Revival by Debendranath Tagore
   a. Group languishes after Roy's death
   b. Debendranath son of Roy's associate Dwarkanath Tagore; members of distinguished Bengali family
   c. Chapters in district towns and cities outside Bengal
   d. Congregational worship, schools, journals
   e. Recruits mainly from high-caste Hindus who tend to inter-marry and live in Brahmo section of Calcutta
   f. Debendranath after scholarly inquiry gives up absolute truth of Vedas (since numerous versions exist)
3. Role of Keshub Sen (1839–1884)
   a. Inspirational preacher recruited by Debendranath
   b. Splits with Debendranath; forms Brahmo Samaj of India
   c. Utilizes Christian and Vaishnavite elements
   d. Second split 1878
      1) Keshub forms Church of the New Dispensation envisioning self as new Christ
      2) Rival group forms Sadharan Brahmo Samaj whose members work at politics and social reform
4. Brahmos as a community
   a. Numerous marriage ties; social and religious functions
   b. Ineffectual outside Bengal: other regions build own groups
C. Ramakrishna, Vivekananda, and the Ramakrishna Mission
   1. Ramakrishna (1836–1886), Bengali Brahman priest
      a. Experiments with variety of religions
         1) Says all paths lead to the one God
         2) Personally finds Mother Goddess most suitable
      b. Serves as inspirational force
         1) Rich sense of parable
         2) Bridges worlds of village and Westernized urban center
   2. Swami Vivekananda (1863–1902), disciple of Ramakrishna
      a. Carries message of revived Hinduism to West
      b. Advocates social work and activist religion
      c. With other disciples forms Ramakrishna Mission
         1) Spreads teachings
         2) Works in education, health
      d. Teachings taken in a political sense by young men
D. Arya Samaj
   1. Founded by Dayananda Saraswati (1824–1883)

2. Advocates return to pristine Hinduism of Vedas
3. Rejects encrustations of later Hinduism and West
4. Popular in Punjab as militant Hindu group
E. Prarthana Samaj
1. Founded in Bombay Presidency, 1867; inspired by Keshub Sen visit
2. Works for social reform
   a. Raising of marriage age
   b. Widow remarriage and release of women from seclusion
3. M.G. Ranade (1852–1904), prominent judge, plays active role
F. Other Hindu organizations
1. Sarvajanik Sabha in Poona
2. Mahajana Sabha in Madras
G. Muslim movements
1. General lag in Western education, but some important cultural movements
2. Wahabi movement
   a. Muslim fundamentalist group with origins in Saudi Arabia
   b. Koran read literally; foreigners threatening
   c. Syed Ahmad of Bareilly (1786–1832), founder in India
      1) To Mecca; then initiates Muslim peasants in Bengal, Bihar
      2) Sets up base in northwest frontier region to fight British
         a) Works in 1820s; killed 1831 or 1832
         b) Movement continues
   d. Program a mixture of the religious, the ethical, the political
      1) Committed to driving foreigners out of India
      2) Sufis condemned as corrupters of Islam
   e. Continues to 1870s
      1) Draws upon peasant resentments
      2) Finally crushed by Government of India
3. Aligarh movement
   a. Founded by Sir Syed Ahmad Khan (1817–1898)
      1) From noble family and in Company service
      2) Defends Muslims against disloyalty charge, especially after 1857
      3) 1875 founds Muhammadan Anglo-Oriental College, Aligarh
   b. Advocates Western education plus Islamic reform
   c. Recruits scions of wealthy Muslims for college
   d. Loyalty to Raj

1) Muslims should stay out of Congress
2) Two-nation theory inappropriately read back into Sir Syed's teachings

e. Opposition to him among orthodox and neo-revivalist Muslims
1) For modernist interpretation of Islam
2) For loyalty to Raj
3) For downgrading Turkish Khilafat

f. Response of Raj helps soften antipathy of Muslims

4. Neo-revivalists (e.g., al-Afghani) advocate ulama-led revival of Islam

Reading Assignments

Chaudhuri, *Autobiography,* book one; book two, chapters 1 and 2
Sources of Indian Tradition, 565–87, 602–59, 739–47; paperback 13–35, 50–107, 187–95

Optional Assignments

Karve, D.D. (ed.). *The New Brahmans. Five Maharashtrian Families.* Berkeley: University of California Press, 1963. Fascinating and useful collection of autobiographies and biographies of important nineteenth-century figures. One gets an inside view of cultural and social reform movements and a sense of the personalities making them.

Ramakrishna. *The Gospel of Sri Ramakrishna.* Recorded by "M," translated by Swami Nikhilananda. Mylapore, Madras: Sri Ramakrishna Math, 1964. The conversation of the Master recorded by his Boswell. One of the most lively and interesting works of modern Indian religious life.

Additional Readings

Levenson, Joseph R. *Liang Ch'i-ch'ao and the Mind of Modern China.* Cambridge: Harvard University Press, 1959 and paperback. Brilliant study of a Chinese figure who is roughly equivalent in importance and time to the Indian figures. Levenson develops the idea of the "need for the conviction of cultural equivalence," which is salient to a consideration of Indian thinkers.

Roy, Rammohun. *The English Works of Raja Rammohun Roy.* Edited by Kalidas Nag and Debajyoti Burman. Five parts. Calcutta: Sàdharan Brahmo Samaj, 1945–1948. Writings on a host of subjects by the important Indian liberal and reformer, who occasionally sounds like his contemporary, John Stuart Mill.

Smith, Wilfred Cantwell. *Modern Islam in India*. Lahore: Sh. Muhammad Ashraf, 1963. Reprint of 1946 edition. A Marxist analysis of Muslim movements which assesses as well as describes the figures and organizations it touches upon. It includes political as well as religious figures.

Discussion Topics and Questions

1. What groups in the population were touched by the Brahmo Samaj? Arya Samaj? Wahabis? Aligarh movement?
2. Analyze the Western and Indian influences in the writings of Rammohun Roy, Ramakrishna, Vivekananda, Dayananda, and Ranade.
3. What were the social, economic, cultural, and political implications of these movements?
4. Compare the Hindu and Muslim cultural movements.

VII. CIVIL RESISTANCE AND 1857

A. General problem
   1. Various types of military, cultural, psychological resistance to British rule
   2. Difficulty in classifying violent outbreaks accompanying and following establishment of British rule
      a. Interpretations relate to investigator's aims, perspectives
      b. Some similarity to revolts against earlier rulers, e.g., Mughals
   3. Possible categories
      a. Native rulers' resistance to British conquest, eighteenth to earlier nineteenth century
         1) Marathas in West
         2) Sikhs in Northwest
      b. Resistance by tribal peoples to British directly or to Hindu exploiters under the Raj (e.g., Santals in Bengal, Bihar, 1860)
      c. Zamindar and peasant resistance to new patterns of revenue collection or to oppression by new landholders (e.g., indigo rebellion in Bengal, 1859–1862)
      d. Army rebellions
         1) Vellore, 1806; Bengal army, 1824; Madras, 1843
         2) Often related to terms of overseas service

3) Fear of being tricked into actions bringing caste or religious sanctions
   e. Problem of labeling such events: mutiny, anarchy, civil disturbances, wars of independence
     1) Related to expansion of Raj
     2) Related to general policies of Raj: doctrine of lapse, army regulations, land revenue policies
B. Events of 1857
  1. Most important of violent resistances
   a. Most significant consequences for later Raj
   b. Effect relationships of Indians and Europeans
  2. Widely varying interpretations of
   a. Degree of planning, organization
   b. Extent and type of population involved
   c. Nature of rebel aims
  3. Fundamental and immediate causes
   a. Implementation of lapse doctrine in Satara, Jhansi, Nagpur, Oudh
   b. Land revenues grievances, e.g., taluqdars, peasants of Oudh
   c. Indian soldiers' (sepoys') grievances about new rifles: greased cartridges, polluting fat (a rumor)
  4. Path of revolt
   a. Precipitating army mutinies
     1) At Barrackpur and Meerut
     2) Meerut soldiers kill officers, march to Delhi, put Mughal scion, Bahadur Shah, on throne
     3) Proclamation issued in name of Mughal emperor: British should be driven out
   b. Following events
     1) Other sepoys revolt, hold Cawnpore, Lucknow
     2) Leaders come forth: Nana Sahib, Rao Sahib, Tantia Topi, Firoz Shah, Rani of Jhansi
     3) Rebels lack systematic plans
     4) Fail to attack Raj at most vulnerable points
   c. Geographic extent of revolt and groups involved
     1) Mainly north and central India
     2) Little support for revolt: coastal Presidencies, among Western-educated, in south, or among Sikhs
     3) Support for revolt: Oudh peasants, landholders; some regiments of Bengal Army; princely states taken over by lapse
   d. British support
     1) Some army regiments and Sikhs recruited for army

      2) Western-educated Indian community

      3) Princes and landholders who see British benefits

    e. British defeat main thrust within several months

      1) Use 40,000 British troops

      2) Search out rebels in inaccessible places during following year

    f. Vicious slaughter of unarmed citizens, prisoners on both sides

      1) British hard on those believed to have murdered European women and children

      2) Slaughter leads to hardening of British racialist attitudes

C. "The Aftermath of Revolt"

  1. Important psychological consequences

    a. Basis of Indian irreconcilability described by Edward Thompson 1920s as due to

      1) Indiscriminate punishments

      2) Glorification of avengers

    b. Latent fears among nonofficials

      1) Slightest stir brings rumor of uprising

      2) Formation of volunteer militias

      3) Argument against arming Indians or training them for warfare

      4) Feeling of living on edge of vast, inhospitable continent

  2. Strong case that policy changes follow revolt

    a. Although generally conservative, more attention to tensions among Indians

    b. Particular instances

      1) Restoration of land rights to aristocracy, especially Punjab, Maharashtra, Oudh

      2) Favoring landlord and moneylender at expense of peasants

      3) Virtual end of annexing princely states

      4) End of government-sponsored social reform: let Indians reform selves

      5) Legislative councils set up to get better sense of local feeling from prominent Indian appointees

      6) Indians allowed to trickle into Indian Civil Service

Reading Assignments

Thompson and Garratt, *Rise and Fulfilment of British Rule,* book V, chapters V, VI; book VI, chapter I

Woodruff, *Men Who Ruled India,* volume I, part III, chapter XII

Optional Assignments

Embree, Ainslee T. (ed.). *1857 in India. Mutiny or War of Independence?* Boston: Heath paperback, 1963. A collection of writings on the revolt which demonstrates the range of interpretations and viewpoints about it. After reading a textbook account, this would be a good second stop.

Metcalf, Thomas R. *The Aftermath of Revolt, India, 1857–1870.* Princeton: Princeton University Press, 1964. Intelligent and well-written account of the consequences of the revolt.

Additional Readings

Chattopadhyaya, Haraprasad. *The Sepoy Mutiny, 1857, A Social Study and Analysis.* Calcutta: Bookland, 1957. A study useful to an understanding of the limitations of the revolt in space and in the elements of the population that were involved.

Chaudhuri, S.B. *Civil Disturbances during the British Rule in India (1765–1857).* Calcutta: The World Press, 1955. A nationalist catalogue of resistances to British rule. Valuable in placing 1857 in the context of a range of revolts over some 90 years.

Hobsbawm, E.J. *Primitive Rebels.* New York: Norton Library, 1965. A lively and suggestive analysis of revolts in Western and Southern Europe which places them in their socioeconomic context. It raises many questions which may be applied to the Indian situation.

Kling, Blair B. *The Blue Mutiny.* Philadelphia: University of Pennsylvania Press, 1966. A skillful account of the rising of indigo cultivators in some Bengal districts during 1859–1862. Their opponents were European planters, and they sought assistance from the British Raj.

Masters, John. *Nightrunners of Bengal.* New York: Bantam paperback, 1962. A lively novel giving the flavor of the revolt of 1857 by the dean of British fictionalizers of India.

Savarkar, Vinayak Damodar. *The Indian War of Independence 1857.* Bombay: Phoenix Publications, 1947. Written in the first decade of this century by a nationalist revolutionary, this tale of the revolt maintains that it was a carefully planned nationalist uprising.

Sen, Surendra Nath. *Eighteen Fifty-Seven.* New Delhi: Publications Division, Government of India, 1957. A sensible, thorough account of the events of 1857 in a volume commissioned by the government. Perhaps the best one-volume account.

Thompson, Edward J. *The Other Side of the Medal.* New York: Harcourt, Brace, 1926. An assessment of the consequences of the revolt of 1857 by a sensitive Englishman filled with the guilt of his people.

Discussion Topics and Questions

1. What criteria might be used in classifying incidents of civil resistance and revolt?
2. Which interpretation of the events of 1857 makes the most sense in terms of the evidence available to you?
3. What were the consequences of 1857 for different groups in the Indian population?
4. Why did certain groups offer their support to the British Raj during 1857?
5. How similar were revolts under the British Raj to those which took place under earlier Indian rulers? (e.g., Mughals) How similar was the response of the British to that of earlier rulers?

VIII. THE BRITISH-INDIAN ESTABLISHMENT AND EARLY NATIONALISM

A. The British-Indian Establishment
   1. Administrative realignments and governmental activities
     a. Company an empty hulk after 1833 charter renewal
     b. Government of India Act, 1858: crown takes over in fact and name
       1) Secretary of State for India and Council of India replace Board of Control
       2) Governor-General now Viceroy too: Crown's representative
       3) Queen Victoria's proclamation at time: equality of opportunity for all citizens
     c. Continuing territorial expansion through nineteenth century
       1) Incorporation of Sind, 1843; of Punjab, 1849
       2) Wars on the frontier: Afghanistan, 1839–1842, 1878–1880
       3) Conquest of Burma: wars, 1824–1826, 1852, 1885–1886; Upper Burma annexed to Raj, 1886; separated, 1937
     d. Army reorganization

      1) Higher ratio of European to Indian troops

      2) Indian artillery disbanded

      3) Limitations on arms for private Indian citizens

   e. Doctrine of paramountcy over Indian states

2. Indian officials hold subordinate positions in Raj

   a. Rulers make groundrules; some Indians seek positions

   b. Limitations on Indian advancement regardless of merit

3. Indian Civil Service and the lower services

   a. Formally Indians can compete for I.C.S.; requirements stacked against them in elite service

   b. A few make it after 1860s

   c. Many Indians in uncovenanted services

4. Legislative Councils and local self-government

   a. Council Acts of 1861 and 1892

      1) Appointees from aristocrats, rural and urban wealthy

      2) Questions asked, but generally councils rubber stamp for Raj

      3) Indirect election and enlargement of councils, 1892

   b. Municipal governing boards in major cities, nineteenth century

      1) Nonofficials, European and Indian, play role

      2) Great variation in effectiveness

   c. Ripon's Local Self-Government Act, 1882

      1) Outlet for Indian aspirations

      2) District Magistrate remained dominant in local government

      3) Change formal; no real power gained

5. Legal institutions

   a. Law Commission established, 1830s

   b. Indian Penal Code, with Codes of Civil and Criminal Procedure, 1860

   c. Supreme Courts for Europeans and Indian courts re-aligned into one system, 1861

   d. High Courts in the Presidencies

   e. Indians as barristers and solicitors following reform

   f. Indians slowly enter European law firms

   g. Some Indians as judges; some lawyers with lucrative practices

6. Educational system

   a. Indians sit on senates of affiliating universities

   b. Indians as vice-chancellors by end of nineteenth century

112

B. Indians in the Establishment
1. Relatively small number of urban Indians associated with Raj
2. Establishment Indians hold several posts simultaneously
   a. Often have numerous personal ties to each other
   b. Bengal: high-caste Hindus dominate, Muslims lag
   c. Bombay: includes some Hindus, Muslims, Parsis
   d. Madras: Brahmans dominate
   e. United Provinces: Muslims do better proportionately
C. Early nationalist organizations and ideology
1. Beginning in regional associations
   a. Bengal: British Indian Association from 1850s and Indian Association from 1870s
   b. Bombay Presidency
      1) Bombay Association, 1852, but languishes later
      2) Bombay Presidency Association, 1885
      3) Poona Sarvajanik Sabha from 1870s; active role of Deccan Brahmans
   c. Madras Native Association, 1840s on, but inactive
   d. Political pressure groups of notables trying to influence regional governments and Raj
   e. Development of native-owned press in regional areas
2. Indian National Congress
   a. Idea of national organization in 1880s
   b. First meeting 1885 in Bombay
      1) Meets annually passing resolutions submitted to government
      2) Little work through year
      3) Run for two decades by small group in Bombay and Calcutta, including Pherozshah Mehta, Dadabhai Naoroji, G.K. Gokhale, Surendranath Banerjea, W.C. Bonnerjee
      4) A few Europeans active, especially Allan O. Hume
   c. Whom did Congress represent?
      1) Claimed to speak for all Indians
      2) Not elected in systematic way; regional associations played key role in selecting delegates
      3) Mostly city men, often lawyers
      4) Muslim participation low
   d. Government response
      1) At first welcomes

113

        2) Soon dampens and Congress called "microscopic minority"
   3. Nationalist ideology
     a. Follows British liberal ideas (e.g., John Stuart Mill)
        1) Self-government by slow steps the goal
        2) Proclaims loyalty to the Raj and adherence to peaceful means
     b. Economic nationalism
        1) Led by Dadabhai Naoroji, Romesh Dutt; argued that India was being drained of wealth for British interests
        2) Wanted governmental help to protect, build Indian economy
     c. Cultural aspects
        1) Wanted regeneration of Indian culture
        2) Some believed India had spiritual message for humanity

Reading Assignments

Sources of Indian Tradition, 660–704; paperback, 108–52
Thompson and Garratt, *Rise and Fulfillment of British Rule,* book VI, chapters II–V; book VII, chapters I–III
Woodruff, *Men Who Ruled India,* volume II, part I

Additional Readings

Banerjea, Surendranath. *A Nation in Making.* Calcutta: Oxford University Press, 1963. Reprint of 1925 edition. Revealing reminiscences of an Indian prominent in politics, education, and journalism for the last quarter of the nineteenth century and the first quarter of the twentieth century. A liberal and an evolutionist, loyal to the Raj, he was displeased by more extreme forms of politics following 1905.

Chandra, Bipin. *The Rise and Growth of Economic Nationalism in India.* New Delhi: People's Publishing House, 1966. A study massive in length and documentation of the views of Indian nationalists about the economic drain, industry, tariffs, agriculture, public finance, trade, etc. in the years 1880 to 1905.

Deutsch, Karl. *Nationalism and Social Communication.* Cambridge: M.I.T. Press paperback, 1966. A stimulating, analytical investigation of the meanings and implications of the concept of nationalism.

Dutt, Romesh. *The Economic History of India under Early British Rule* and *The Economic History of India in the Victorian Age.* London: Routledge and Kegan Paul, 1956. The most systematic and clearly written presentation of the drain theory by a talented I.C.S. officer and early nationalist.

Kipling, Rudyard. "The Enlightenments of Pagett, M.P.," "The Head of the District," and "The City of Dreadful Night," in *Selected Prose and Poetry of Rudyard Kipling*. Garden City, New York: Garden City Publishing Company, 1937. Savage, satirical descriptions of the failures of Indians as I.C.S. members and politicians, embodied in short stories and a travelogue by the doyen of British writers on India.

Philips, C.H. (ed.). *The Evolution of India and Pakistan, 1858–1947, Select Documents*. London: Oxford University Press, 1962. See the documents on the latter nineteenth century.

Seal, Anil. *The Emergence of Indian Nationalism*. Cambridge: Cambridge University Press, 1968. A valuable synthesis on Indian society, education, and politics at the beginning of the nationalist period.

Discussions Topics and Questions

1. Why did Indians serve in the British-Indian establishment? What limitations were placed on their advancement?
2. What were the social backgrounds of the members and leaders of the early political associations?
3. How did early nationalists reconcile British rule with their desire for Indian self-government?
4. What were the economic bases of Indian nationalism?
5. What was the power structure of the early Indian National Congress?
6. Analyze the changing government attitude towards the Congress.

IX. CURZON'S RAJ AND THE SWADESHI MOVEMENT

A. Government of India under Lord Curzon, Viceroy, 1899–1905
   1. Faltering of small steps towards self-government that were associated with Lord Ripon and British Liberalism
   2. More authoritarian rule associated with Lord Curzon's regime
      a. Curzon's aim of rationalizing, improving administration from above
      b. Steps towards confrontation with incipient nationalism

      1) Calcutta Municipal Act of 1899 cuts back Indian participation in Calcutta city affairs; most Indian members resign

      2) Indian Education Act, 1904
        a) Curzon writes act bringing affiliated colleges more directly under governmental supervision
        b) Objections from Indian political and cultural leaders like Rabindranath Tagore

      3) Partition of Bengal, 1905
        a) Large Bengal Presidency severed into western section with Hindu majority and Eastern Bengal and Assam with Muslim majority
        b) Bengali-speaking people in both new provinces
        c) Government gives administrative rationale and denies political motivation
        d) Top officials privately admit aim of curbing vocal Bengali nationalist politicians

B. Nationalist currents and responses
  1. Later nineteenth century: self-help and nativist ideology, activity
    a. Tilak's work in Maharashtra; Shivaji festivals
    b. Hindu Mela in Bengal
    c. Self-strengthening, activist theme in writings of Bankim Chandra Chatterjee, Dayananda, Vivekananda, Tilak
  2. First nationalist response
    a. Unity against the government in calling for revocation of partition
    b. Entry of older, apolitical men, students, religiously-tinged extreme elements into political arena
    c. Bengal momentarily the cynosure of Indian politics
  3. Narrow and extensive programs within the movement
    a. Limited steps advocated by Surendranath Banerjea and Moderates of Congress establishment: temporary boycott against partition
    b. Rabindranath Tagore's proposal for a "Swadeshi Samaj"
      1) Self-help at all levels of the society led initially by nationalists and students
      2) Tagore urged bridging of gap between Westernized, urban India and rural, peasant India
      3) Plans not implemented
    c. Political program of Extremist leader Aurobindo Ghose (1872–1950)
      1) Emerges from obscurity to formulate views in "Doc-

trine of Passive Resistance" and other articles and speeches

  2) Advocates mass movement ignoring government and setting up Indian educational, legal, political, economic institutions

  3) Approves use of violence when possible and appropriate

  4) Extremists Tilak and Ghose express confluence of nineteenth-century religious revivalist currents and nationalist politics

 d. Boycott of British goods

  1) Practical work done by students is effective around Calcutta for a few months

  2) Effectiveness rapidly declines; no enduring organization for boycott and political activity built

4. Divisions in the movement

 a. Moderates versus Extremists

  1) Conflict over goals, program, control of Congress organization first surfaces in 1906

  2) Split at Surat Congress, 1907

  3) Rump Congress of Moderates continues into World War I

  4) Extremists suffer government repression, lack of staying power and temporary fade from scene

 b. Muslim politics and the Muslim League

  1) Government labors to get support for partition among Muslims in East Bengal

  2) Muslim opposition to partition and support for Congress exists only weakly

  3) Government and Muslim initiative leads to formation of Muslim League, 1906

  4) League is small group of notables claiming to speak for entire Muslim community

  5) League men lobby in Calcutta, London (as Congressmen do)

 c. Revolutionary movement

  1) Begins late nineteenth century in Maharashtra: murder of British official by Chapekar brothers

  2) Spread in early twentieth century to Bengal, Punjab

  3) Actions mostly assassinations of officials and robberies to finance work

  4) Large-scale plot to rise against Raj in Bengal

   a) Through contacts abroad German aid secured during World War I

        b) Government's intelligence network snaps plot

    5) Ghadr Party of Punjabis including foreign returnees

    6) Government repression effective by end of World War I

C. Government reactions

  1. Morley-Minto reforms, 1909

    a. Legislative councils expanded, greater number elected

    b. Separate electorates for Muslims

      1) Pushed by League, Minto

      2) Long-range consequences of communal electorates not foreseen

    c. Limited powers of councilors, especially over budget

    d. Moderates welcome reforms though want more

    e. Extremists mock reforms as worthless tokens

  2. Bengal partition revocation, 1912: Bengali-speaking peoples reunited

    a. Congressmen see shift as result of peaceful agitation

    b. Many articulate Muslim writers, politicians call revocation a betrayal

    c. Capital of British India shifted to Delhi from Calcutta as part of same government action

Reading Assignments

Brown, *United States and India and Pakistan,* chapter 4

Chaudhuri, *Autobiography,* book two, chapter 3

Sources of Indian Tradition, 705–38; paperback, 153–86

Thompson and Garratt, *Rise and Fulfilment of British Rule,* book VII, chapters IV–V

Additional Readings

Chirol, Valentine. *Indian Unrest.* London: Macmillan, 1910. Lively British analysis of the rise of the Extremists in Indian politics. Chirol was an advocate of the theory that a few deranged Brahmans were endangering British rule in India.

Ghose, Aurobindo. *The Doctrine of Passive Resistance.* Pondicherry: Sri Aurobindo Ashram, 1948. Sharply written and well-argued rationale for a subject people's use of both violence and mass nonviolent resistance, according to what circumstances dictate. The author was a Congress leader, journalist, and secret revolutionary.

Gordon, Leonard A. "Portrait of a Bengal Revolutionary," *Journal of Asian Studies,* XXVII, no. 2 (February, 1968), 197–216. Analysis of the organization and leadership of revolutionary groups.

Ronaldshay, Earl of. *The Life of Lord Curzon.* Volume II. London: Ernest Benn, 1928. Elegantly written and insightful official biography of the great and infamous Viceroy. This volume covers the years in India. The author served as Governor of Bengal and later Secretary of State for India.

Tinker, Hugh. *Foundations of Local Self-Government in India, Pakistan and Burma*. New York: Praeger, 1968. Important study of the slow development of rural, district, and municipal governments in South Asia. The author analyzes the reasons for the weakness of these institutions before the 1920s.

Wolpert, Stanley A. *Tilak and Gokhale*. Berkeley: University of California Press, 1962. Valuable and detailed study which contrasts the two leading figures from Maharashtra who were in the forefront of Indian politics from the 1890s through the 1910s. The author argues that the traditions these men embodied, reform and revolution, were combined by Gandhi after World War I.

Discussion Topics and Questions

1. Analyze Lord Curzon's views of Indian society and politics. Relate them to his own biography and to the cultural and political currents in Britain and India during the nineteenth century. Compare Curzon's ideology and actions with those of Lord Morley and Lord Minto.
2. How does the Swadeshi movement relate to cultural and religious currents in nineteenth-century India?
3. Compare Tilak and Surendranath Banerjea as political leaders.
4. Was there an economic basis for the unrest during the Swadeshi period?
5. Why weren't Muslims and peasants more directly involved in the Swadeshi movement?
6. What economic, social, political, and cultural forces generated the revolutionary movement in India during the first two decades of this century?

X. INDIAN INTELLECTUAL LIFE AND THE CAREER OF RABINDRANATH TAGORE

A. Traditional role of the learned man, poet, artist
  1. Financed by patrons among wealthy and powerful
  2. Reformers, social critics more often in religious context, e.g., Buddhists, bhakti poets, Sikhs

B. Changing economic, social, cultural context of British Raj
   1. Decline of older forms of patronage
   2. Western as well as Indian models for critic, intellectual, artist
   3. Development of new cultural forms and new means of communication
   4. Beginnings of writer, artist communication with mass audience
   5. Limited opportunity for writer and artist to make a living by creations alone, but some do
C. Continuing dilemmas
   1. Alienation from Indian society, especially rural society
      a. Tendency to discuss peasant problems abstractly without concrete experience
      b. Theme of discovery of rural India, e.g., Nehru's autobiography, *Toward Freedom*
   2. Relationships to Hindu traditions
      a. Learn of great traditional works of Hinduism through Western translations
      b. Attempts to synthesize Western and Indian elements into new and relevant wholes
   3. Relationship to politics and civic responsibility
      a. Many participate in nationalist movement
      b. "Dirtier" politics, e.g., municipal affairs, ignored
D. The career and achievements of Rabindranath Tagore (1861–1941)
   1. Background
      a. Tagores one of the leading families of Bengal
      b. Family members explore religion and the arts (literature, music, visual arts) in nineteenth century
      c. Rabindranath youngest son of religious reformer Debendranath
      d. Family members encourage experimentation, freedom
      e. Wealthy setting gives Rabindranath and other Tagores leisure to pursue cultural interests
   2. Growth
      a. Amidst resurgent cultural activity in Bengal, Rabindranath blossoms as a poet in the 1870s and 1880s
      b. He experiments with a variety of literary forms
         1) Creates a number of freer verse forms and plays with imitations of sixteenth-century Vaishnava poetry
         2) Writes diaries bringing spoken and written Bengali together; uses simpler prose

c. Sent to work on family estates in rural East Bengal
  1) Discovers Indian peasants and their problems
  2) Begins writing wonderful, engaging short stories of peasants and rural life
d. Develops keener sense of political, cultural, social responsibility for his people in 1890s
3. Maturity
  a. An early school dropout, he turns attention to educational questions as lifelong special concern
    1) Presses for education at all levels in vernacular language and for downgrading of education through English
    2) Advocates freer, unregimented education, preferably in rural setting
    3) Wants education of peasants partly through their own cultural, oral traditions; e.g., folk plays
    4) Founds school for young children at Santiniketan, rural West Bengal, in 1901; concrete implementation of his educational ideas
    5) Prepares textbooks for learning Bengali, English, science
    6) Santiniketan transformed in 1920s into Vishva-Bharati University with teachers, scholars, students from many countries
  b. Political involvement and detachment
    1) Most active in nationalist politics 1890s through Swadeshi period (to 1908)
    2) Believes in peaceful work outside scope of Raj, organizing society from urban center to village peripheries
    3) Wants sense of self-help fostered in peasants after urban contact
    4) Leader of anti-partition agitation
    5) Disturbed by lack of Hindu-Muslim rapport and advocates more attention to problem
    6) Critic of weak petitioners and revolutionaries
      a) Claims both seek shortcuts to true Indian revival
      b) In turn, Tagore much criticized
    7) Withdraws from direct involvement but continues to write insightfully on political questions rest of life
  c. Nobel Prize winner and spokesman to the West
    1) 1912 wins Nobel Prize for *Gitanjali;* first Asian so recognized
    2) Thereafter makes extensive journeys to many countries

121

       3) Serves as spokesman for Indian culture, religion

       4) More Indian in the West, more Western in India

  d. Critic of Gandhi and Indian nationalism in 1920s

       1) Contrasts variety of paths to fulfillment with what he sees as Gandhi's more unitary, authoritarian views

       2) Gandhi's thoughtful response: bread and work before poetry

       3) Respectful relationship to Gandhi, warmer tie to Jawaharlal Nehru

  e. 1930s takes up painting

  f. Visits Soviet Union, 1930

       1) Impressed with progress in education, reviving masses

       2) Critical of some authoritarian features, but sees useful example for India

  g. Final word: "Crisis in Civilization," 1941

       1) Europe still bankrupt

       2) India lags and must revive

Reading Assignments

Sources of Indian Tradition, 782–99; paperback, 230–47

Optional Assignments

Shils, Edward. *The Intellectual between Tradition and Modernity. The Indian Situation.* The Hague: Mouton, 1961. A stimulating and opinionated essay based on intensive interviews with a sample of Indian intellectuals. The author found Indians still tied to the standards of the imperial metropolitan center rather than setting out more autonomously and adventurously.

Tagore, Rabindranath. *The Housewarming.* New York: Signet paperback, 1965. A collection of stories, plays, and poems which serves as a good introduction to Tagore's writing. The translations are rather literal.

Additional Readings

Chaudhuri, Nirad C. *The Intellectual in India.* New Delhi: Vir Publishing House, 1967. A lively series of essays by India's foremost intellectual on the problems of survival and creativity in an arid environment.

Kripalani, Krishna. *Rabindranath Tagore: A Biography.* New York: Grove Press, 1961. Smoothly written and insightful biography which is especially good on Tagore's life and poetry during his first five decades.

122

Tagore, Rabindranath. *Towards Universal Man*. New York: Asia Publishing House, 1961. A valuable volume of Tagore's essays on political, cultural, social, and educational questions. There are some unfortunate and unnoted abridgments made by the editors, but nonetheless this is a useful and well-translated collection.

Tagore, Rabindranath. *A Tagore Reader*. Edited by Amiya Chakravarty. New York: Macmillan, 1961 and paperback. An introduction to Tagore which contains short selections from all the different genres which he explored.

Tagore, Rabindranath. "The Religion of an Artist," in *Rabindranath Tagore on Art and Aesthetics*. New Delhi: Orient Longmans, 1961. An autobiographical essay in which Tagore sees himself as part of three rebel traditions in nineteenth-century Indian culture.

Discussion Topics and Questions

1. Assess Edward Shils' view of the Indian intellectual.
2. Discuss the similarities and dissimilarities between the traditional and modern man of letters in India.
3. Analyze the participation of Indian men of letters in Indian nationalism.
4. In what ways was Rabindranath Tagore both alienated from and intensely involved in Indian society?
5. Discuss the relationship of Tagore's ideas and literary experiments to Western currents of ideas and literature.

XI. MODERN LITERATURE AND THE ARTS

A. Literature in the nineteenth and twentieth centuries
   1. "Modernization" of Indian literature: British rule and contacts with European culture provide the environment
      a. Introduction of the printing press: challenge to the oral tradition
      b. English education
         1) British literary taste: romantic poetry, novels; Shakespeare
         2) Access to other Western literature, mainly through English translations

3) Transmission of Western literary and sociological ideas: e.g., political influence of Marxism from 1920s

    c. Rise of new literati; uncommitted to traditional formalism, at same time discovering immensity and variety of ancient literary heritage; internationalism and nationalism

2. Literary trends which characterize modern literature in most Indian languages

    a. Emergence of prose as a major medium (vs. traditional dominance of poetry); development of the novel and the short story

    b. Introduction of social and psychological issues as literary themes

        1) Impact on rural India of cultural revival and nationalism; influence of Gandhi's writing and teaching

        2) Alienation and discovery: self, traditions, country

    c. Acceptance of realism as literary technique: characters from all levels of society; representation of the hardships of Indian life (vs. traditional idealizations of characters and settings)

    d. Individualistic expression and imagery, symbolism in poetry; experimental forms, often based on folk traditions

3. Linguistic diversity: the polyglot nature of Indian literature

    a. Local mythology, literary forms in the various vernacular languages; regional versions of Sanskrit works; degrees of foreign influence

    b. Uneven developments: Bengali and Hindi literatures dominate the modern scene in quantity and quality; important works in every major language, including English

    c. Problems of translating works from one language into the others

4. Examples of prose and poetry in Bengali, Hindi-Urdu, English

    a. Bengali: the role Rammohun Roy; dominating figure of Tagore (see X above)

        1) Poetry: Michael Madhusudan Datta's epic and lyric forms; experiments of Tagore and successors, e.g., Sudhin Datta, Bishnu Dey, Jibanananda Das, Nazrul Islam; influence of Western poets like Eliot and Pound and of Marxist thought

        2) Fiction: Bankim Chandra Chatterji develops the novel form; works of Tagore, Sarat Chandra Chatterjee, Bib-

    hutibhusan Banerji, Manik Bandopadhyay, Tarasankar
    Banerji

  b. Hindi-Urdu: with dialectal variants is the basic language
    of Northern India; Urdu developed as language of mili-
    tary camp and bazaar, uses Arabic and Persian vocabulary
    and literary forms; Hindi uses Sanskritized vocabulary and
    literary forms

    1) Poetry: Urdu ghazals of Ghalib; philosophic Urdu
       poetry of Muhammed Iqbal; romantic Hindi poetry of
       Sumitranandan Pant, Nirala; experimental works of
       Agyeya

    2) Fiction: Premchand, storyteller of the Indian indepen-
       dence movement, *Godan* (*Gift of a Cow*); successors in-
       clude Yashpal, Agyeya, Mohan Rakesh

  c. English: related to regional developments, but directed to
    a different audience; Indian-English, effect of using a
    "foreign" medium for creative writing

    1) Little innovation in poetry

    2) Fiction: outstanding works in various styles; Mulk Raj
       Anand, R.K. Narayan, Raja Rao, Khushwant Singh,
       Bhabhani Bhattacharya, G.V. Desani

    3) Nonfiction: autobiographies of Jawaharlal Nehru,
       Nirad C. Chaudhuri

B. Fine Arts: revival of ancient themes and techniques, combined
  with Western styles, new techniques

  1. Individual artists: Abaninranath Tagore, Jamini Roy, Amrita
    Sher Gil

  2. Folk art and handicrafts: national support, wider audience
    (related situations in music, dance)

C. Indian films

  1. Films as a major mode of mass communication in a largely
    illiterate population; the film industry and its vast audience

  2. The achievements of Satyajit Ray

    a. Use of Indian literature, music

    b. Traditional and modern themes and elements

    c. Indian and Western audience response

Reading Assignments

Rao, Raja. *Kanthapura*. London: Allen and Unwin, 1938. New
  Directions paperback, 1967. A novel in English about the impact
  of the Indian independence movement on a traditional South

Indian village. Interesting blend of traditional and modern literary techniques and themes.

Shimer, Dorothy Blair. *The Mentor Book of Modern Asian Literature*. New York: New American Library, 1969, Pp. 25–55, 276–95, 323–41; examples of Indian poetry, short story, novel.

Sources of Indian Tradition, 587–601, 707–17, 751–58; paperback, 35–49, 155–65, 199–206

Additional Readings

LITERARY WORKS

Banerji, Bibhutibhusan. *Pather Panchali*. Translated by T.W. Clark and Tarapada Mukherji. Bloomington: Indiana University Press, 1968. Good translation of the Bengali novel which served as the basis for Satyajit Ray's film.

Ghalib. *Ghazals of Ghalib*. Edited by Alijaz Ahmad. New York: Columbia University Press, 1971. A translation experiment sponsored by the Asia Society. Contains selected stanzas in Urdu, literal translations prepared by the editor, and transcreations by seven well-known poets prepared from the translations.

Kabir, Humayun (ed.). *Green and Gold: Stories and Poems from Bengal*. New York: New Directions, 1958. Best collection of post-Tagore Bengali literature.

Mahfil: A Quarterly of South Asian Literature. South Asia Center, University of Chicago. General and special issues on writers and regional literature; includes new translations of many stories and poems as well as articles.

Misra, V.N. (ed.). *Modern Hindi Poetry*. Bloomington: Indiana University Press, 1968. Transcreations of Hindi poetry by American poets.

Narayan, R.K. *The Financial Expert*. New York: Noonday Press paperback, 1959. One of the best of Narayan's novels about the fictional South Indian town of Malgudi and its inhabitants.

Nehru, Jawaharlal. *Towards Freedom*. Boston: Beacon paperback, 1958. The autobiography of an important Congress leader who became India's prime minister and a world figure. It comes up to 1935 and gives a passionate and vivid account of the resurgence of the Congress in the 1920s and 1930s and of the author's relationship to Gandhi.

Premchand. *The Gift of a Cow*. Translated by C. Gordon Roadarmel. Bloomington: Indiana University Press, 1968. Paperback,

1970. A fine translation of Premchand's celebrated novel of economic and social conflict in a North Indian Village.

Premchand. *The World of Premchand*. Translated by David Rubin. Bloomington: Indiana University Press, 1969. Selected stories in excellent translations.

SECONDARY SOURCES

Barnouw, Erik, and S. Krishnaswamy. *Indian Film*. New York: Columbia University Press, 1953. A history and assessment.

Bussabarger, Robert F., and Betty Dashew Robins. *The Everyday Art of India*. New York: Dover paperback, 1968. Works classified by materials and techniques; profusely illustrated.

Chatterji, Suniti Kumar. *Languages and Literatures of Modern India*. Calcutta: Bengal Publishers, 1963. Scholarly introduction to linguistic and literary background of modern Indian literature.

Rao, Ramachandra. *Modern Indian Painting*. Madras: Rachana, 1953. A survey of movements and painters; well illustrated.

Spencer, Dorothy. *Indian Fiction in English: An Annotated Bibliography*. Philadelphia: University of Pennsylvania Press, 1960. Contains an introductory essay on Indian society, culture, and fiction, and an annotated list of fictional and autobiographical works written in and translated into English.

Swan, Robert O. *Munshi Premchand of Lamhi Village*. Durham: Duke University Press, 1969. Critical and biographical analysis of the development of Premchand's style and concerns.

Discussion Topics and Questions

1. What do the settings, cultural traditions, and values which recur in works of modern Indian fiction tell us about India?
2. To what audiences is modern Indian literature addressed in the regional languages and in English?
3. How are the novel, essay, and autobiography related to earlier Indian literary forms? Discuss experiments in literature of various languages.
4. How have literary developments been related to the rise of Indian nationalism?
5. Discuss the themes of alienation, protest, and resignation in modern Indian literature. What is the significance of the relation between village and city in the development of these themes?

6. Analyze the attempts of modern painters to create distinctively Indian styles of painting in terms of subject and technique.
7. Discuss the multiple roles of the film in India.

XII. PROCESSES OF SOCIAL, ECONOMIC, AND EDUCATIONAL CHANGE, NINETEENTH AND TWENTIETH CENTURY

A. Demographic change and urbanization
  1. Indian census from 1872
     a. Can more precisely calculate growth regardless of errors
     b. Figures: 1872, 255 million; 1901, 285 million; 1921, 306 million; 1941, 389 million
  2. More rapid growth after 1921
     a. Population rises three times as fast as total agricultural output rises, 1893 to 1946
     b. Threatens positive economic development
  3. Slow, steady growth of urban percentage of population
     a. Difficulties in defining "urban": sometimes means those in units of 5,000 or more
     b. Growth of industrial centers in and near major cities and nearer to natural resources; e.g., Jamshedpur
B. Economic enterprise and industrialization
  1. Government policy
     a. Laissez-faire or night watchman attitude: no active program for economic development
     b. Slow shift from protection for British industries to some protection for Indian ones after World War I
  2. Managing agency system from earlier nineteenth century
     a. Diversity of enterprises joined under one agency roof
     b. Advantages: capital from number of sources utilized; central office for large number of enterprises
     c. Disadvantages: juggling of accounts more possible; when many enterprises joined, mismanagement easier
     d. Mainly European; by World War II, gains made by Indian firms, especially those headed by Parsis and Marwaris
  3. Growth of chambers of commerce in nineteenth century which present business viewpoint to government
     a. European chambers: Bengal Chamber of Commerce, 1834; also Madras and Bombay chambers

  b. Indian chambers: Bengal National Chamber of Commerce, 1887; Marwari Association of Calcutta, 1898

  c. By 1930s foreign and native businessmen join against government and later Indian Government encroachments

 4. Growth of industry and commerce

  a. Growth of substantial cotton textile, jute, coal mining, railway industries by World War I

   1) Leading role of Scotsmen in jute, Indians in textiles

   2) Leading sectors do not pull rest of economy into sustained industrial revolution

  b. Increased foreign and domestic commerce

C. Labor recruitment and unions

 1. Arguments on labor recruitment

  a. Caste and rural ties hinder recruiting of industrial workers

  b. Reply and systematic data of economic historian Morris D. Morris

   1) Bombay cotton mills, 1870–1920, little problem recruiting

   2) Members of different jatis work together in factories

   3) All' clean-caste Hindus and all untouchables lumped into two separate categories

   4) With more untouchables employed segregation slowly erodes

   5) Tata Iron and Steel, Jamshedpur: stable labor force

 2. Trade unions

  a. Significant development after World War I, especially in Bombay, Calcutta, Ahmadabad

  b. Great strikes in 1920s

   1) Many unions not strong enough to withstand pressures

   2) Political combat for control of unions in Congress, among communist, socialist organizers

  c. 1930s: cutback in industrial production which unions cannot prevent

D. Trends on the land

 1. Expansion of cultivated area

  a. Increased regional specialization of crops

  b. Irrigation works, especially in Punjab

  c. More commercial agriculture

  d. Slow growth in agricultural output, which some call stagnation

   1) Growth mostly in commercial crops: cotton, peanuts, tobacco, sugarcane

2) Some studies show food production down slightly, 1893–1946
    e. Increased pressure on the land
  2. Golden age of moneylenders in the countryside
  3. Cooperative movement begins early twentieth century to provide better, less exploitative source of credit
  4. Growth in number, perhaps percentage of landless laborers
E. Social organization and social mobility
  1. Class and caste
    a. One suggestion: rural caste, urban class overlap; latter based on achievement and general movement towards class society
    b. Further suggestion: class coming to villages
      1) Based on role in production
      2) Class, caste more differentiated with movement from closed to more open social system
    c. Definitions of class do not mention class consciousness as crucial element (follow Max Weber rather than Karl Marx)
  2. Westernization and Sanskritization
    a. Both processes continue as vehicles of social mobility; can bring change of position but not basic structural change of the society
    b. Both may take place in single village as upper group Westernizes, lower group Sanskritizes
    c. Other cultural avenues to mobility, e.g., untouchables become Buddhists in western India
  3. Social reform efforts
    a. Missionaries work among tribal groups: bring Western education, health services, Christianity
    b. Beginning of government help to "Scheduled Castes and Tribes"
      1) Reserved places in legislatures; later in education, services
      2) Possibilities for rise in status, improvement of power position especially after independence
F. Education
  1. Growth in absolute numbers of educated continues though literacy percentage still low
  2. Improvement in engineering, law, medical, scientific education
  3. Growing number of educated unemployed
    a. Some see them related to growing nationalism, discontent

130

b. Lack of clarity in such generalizations
   1) Overestimate role of unemployed in nationalism
   2) Underestimate importance of legitimate political grievances

Reading Assignments

Chaudhuri, *Autobiography,* book three

Thompson and Garratt, *Rise and Fulfilment of British Rule,* book VII, chapter VI

Optional Assignments

Morris, Morris David. *The Emergence of an Industrial Labor Force in India. A Study of the Bombay Cotton Mills, 1854–1947.* Berkeley: University of California, 1966. An excellent analytical study of developments in the textile industry in Bombay which deals with the problems of labor recruitment, mobility, organization, discipline, and wages in a most sophisticated manner.

Thorner, Daniel and Alice. *Land and Labour in India.* Bombay: Asia Publishing House, 1962. A valuable collection of articles on Indian society and economy which questions governmental assessments (under British rule and under independent Indian rule) of economic development and of shifts in landholding due to land reform.

Additional Readings

Buchanann, D.H. *The Development of Capitalistic Enterprise in India.* Reprint of 1934 edition. London: Frank Cass, 1966. An old, but still useful study which surveys the development of industries, labor, and commercial agriculture and the organization of the firms involved into the 1930s.

Karve, D.C. (ed.). *The New Brahmans.* Berkeley: University of California, 1966.

Morris, Morris David. "Towards a Reinterpretation of Nineteenth Century Indian Economic History." *The Journal of Economic History,* XXIII (December, 1963) 606–18. A suggestive article which raises a host of questions for future research and expresses skepticism about simple nationalist interpretations of India's recent economic history.

Neale, Walter C. *Economic Change in Rural India, Land Tenure and Reform in Uttar Pradesh, 1800–1955.* New Haven: Yale University Press, 1962. A study of changes in land holding and the rural economy in Uttar Pradesh from the Mughal period to the present. The author argues that the stagnation in rural India is partly due to the incomplete transformation of the formerly self-sufficient village economy into a sector of the modern market economy.

Srinivas, M.N. *Social Change in Modern India.* See Optional Assignments, V.

Discussion Topics and Questions

1. To what extent did the British transform India into a colonial economy appended to and exploited by the parent country?
2. Are Indians deficient in the economic skills necessary to build a modern economy?
3. Assess the urban-rural and industrial-agricultural balance at different points in time during the last two centuries.
4. Discuss the possibilities for and the barriers against social change and social mobility in India during the last two centuries.

XIII. MAHATMA GANDHI AND THE DEVELOPMENT OF THE CONGRESS

A. World War I and Indian politics
   1. Congress Moderates support government efforts with "heart and soul"
   2. Britain's worldwide intelligence network successfully combats Indian revolutionary activity
   3. Rise of Home Rule Leagues led by Tilak and Annie Besant, 1916
      a. Tilak works in Maharashtra, Karnataka; Besant rest of India
      b. Many branches formed doing propaganda, educational, organizing work
      c. Go into previously less active areas: south, United Provinces
      d. Pressure on Congress Moderates for more militancy
      e. Challenge for Congress control
         1) Unsuccessful attempt to take over organization
         2) Congress in unstable, leaderless situation, 1917–1919; Moderates moving out; Extremists have not yet taken over

132

4. Rapprochement between Muslim League and Congress, 1916
    a. Politically active Muslims move away from loyalism
    b. League and Congress leaders moving closer; meet at Lucknow
    c. Lucknow Pact
        1) Congress accepts separate electorates for Muslims
        2) Muslims get fewer seats in majority areas and more in minority areas than population figures dictate
5. Edwin Montagu, Secretary of State for India, tours India, 1917
    a. Meets Indian leaders to plan further steps to self-government
    b. Montagu's declaration: "progressive realisation of responsible government in India" an aim (August 1917)
B. Rise of Mahatma Gandhi (1869–1948)
    1. Background
        a. From Vaishya family; Kathiawar, Gujarat area; family members prominent in state service
        b. Vaishnava, Jain influences in family, local culture
        c. To England, 1888
            1) Called to bar after rigorous studies
            2) Experiments with Western culture rejected in favor of vegetarianism, ascetic lifestyle
        d. A professional failure in India
    2. Offered a position and goes to South Africa, 1893, where he finds himself
        a. More successful professionally
        b. Finds true calling as leader of Indian community in pursuit of social justice through nonviolent means
        c. Influenced by Tolstoy, Thoreau, Christ, Ruskin, and Hindu texts
        d. Calls method of truth-seeking and change Satyagraha (Sanskrit: grasped by the truth)
        e. Rules for Satyagrahis include suffering, love for opponents, chastity, devotion to cause
        f. In conflict situation successively greater pressures on opponent through nonviolent means
        g. Elevation of nonviolent means (adherence to ahimsa) to even greater importance than goals sought
        h. Experimental communities: Phoenix Settlement, Tolstoy Farm
    3. Return to India, 1915

133

a. Ties to Congress Moderate leader G.K. Gokhale
b. First efforts at applying methods in India
   1) Champaran: Bihar peasant movement, 1917
   2) Ahmadabad: textile workers strike, 1918
C. Noncooperation and Congress reorganization
   1. Gandhi moves to the fore in nationalist politics, 1918–1920
      a. Shifts from cooperator with government to noncooperator with Rowlatt bills (repressive measures)
      b. Leads nationwide agitation against Rowlatt bills
      c. Slaughter of unarmed Indians in Jallianwallah Bagh, Amritsar, Punjab, April 1919
      d. Gandhi on Congress inquiry commission
   2. Gandhi's campaign to capture control of Congress, 1919–1921
      a. Travels country advocating nonviolent noncooperation
      b. Gains converts, supporters throughout India
      c. Wins majority for his program
      d. Support of Indian Muslims on Khilifat issue gains Gandhi and Congress their temporary and wholehearted cooperation
   3. Nationwide noncooperation, 1921–1922
      a. Redress of grievances about Punjab massacre, Khilafat issue, and "swaraj," the three bases of campaign
      b. Swaraj means self-government to some, but vaguer general meaning to Gandhi
      c. Critics of Gandhi's program include Tagore, Bipin Pal; also former Congress Moderates, now Liberals
      d. Gandhi uses campaign to revitalize Congress
         1) Congress reorganized by linguistic regions
         2) Working Committee or executive of Congress formed
         3) Low dues and concerted mass membership drive
         4) Extensive and successful fund-raising, especially among businessmen in western India
      e. Murders at Chauri Chaura and Gandhi calls off movement, 1922
D. Montagu-Chelmsford reforms and government policy
   1. Government of India Act, 1919
      a. Increase in size of and electorate for legislative councils
      b. Dyarchy: nation-building departments of provincial governments, with Indian ministers
         1) Reserved powers for provincial governors and center
         2) More direct concern of legislators with budget, but no control

2. Responses to the Act and its implementation
   a. Liberals accept terms and stand for seats
   b. Congress boycotts elections, 1920
   c. Early, limited successes of Act and Indian ministers
      1) Hampered by scarcity of funds for nation-building
      2) All legislators desirous of more power
E. Swaraj Party
   1. Alternative strategy of group within Congress from 1922
      a. New proposals put forth after Gandhi's cancellation of noncooperation
      b. Motilal Nehru and C.R. Das advocate blocking legislative councils from within
      c. Gandhi imprisoned by government, but his supporters oppose new line
      d. Nehru and Das head Swaraj Party
         1) Conflict with Gandhians, or No-Changers, within Congress
         2) Election campaign and successes, 1923
         3) Swarajists block ministerial salaries and budget items in Bengal
         4) Come to parity with No-Changers within Congress
         5) Also effective in Central Legislature
         6) Das dies 1925 and Swarajist effectiveness declines
F. Reconsiderations, late 1920s
   1. Parliamentary commission to consider working of 1919 Act
      a. Simon Commission constituted without Indian members
      b. Most Indian political groups boycott it
      c. Commission tours India and reports on shortcomings of reforms
   2. Indian organizations hold All-Parties Conference, 1928
      a. Nehru Report formulated with Congress ideas for advancement
      b. Liberals and Muslim League decline to support it

Reading Assignments

Brecher, *Nehru,* chapters I–IV
Brown, *United States and India and Pakistan,* chapter 5
Chaudhuri, *Autobiography,* book four
Sources of Indian Tradition, 768–81, 799–836; paperback 216–29
Thompson and Garratt, *Rise and Fulfilment of British Rule,* book VIII

Woodruff, *Men Who Ruled India,* volume II, part II, chapters I–III

Optional Assignments

Bondurant, Joan. *The Conquest of Violence.* Berkeley: University of California Press paperback, 1959. The best brief, analytical account of several of the important Gandhian satyagraha campaigns; a lucid exposition of Gandhi's philosophy which traces its Indian roots.

Lewis, Martin Deming (ed.). *Gandhi, Maker of Modern India?* Boston: Heath paperback, 1965. A very useful collection of articles about Gandhi, many of them critical, by Indian Marxists, Hindu Nationalists, and Europeans.

Additional Readings

Broomfield, J.H. *Elite Conflict in a Plural Society.* Berkeley: University of California, 1968. A valuable study of Bengal politics covering the period 1912 to 1927 in detail. Very critical of extreme nationalists and revolutionaries, the author tends to identify with British Liberals and Indian Moderates. There are interesting sections on Bengali Muslim politics.

Erikson, Erik H. *Gandhi's Truth.* New York: Norton paperback, 1969. A recent and widely acclaimed study of Gandhi by a prominent psychologist. Erikson concentrates his investigation on the Ahmadabad textile strike of 1917–1918, which he calls "The Event." There are valuable sections dealing with Gandhi's skillful recruitment of supporters and with Gandhi's childhood.

Gandhi, M.K. *An Autobiography, The Study of My Experiments with Truth.* Boston: Beacon Press paperback, 1957. A revealing and interesting account of Gandhi's life into the 1920s. Although the individual chapters were written serially for didactic purposes, a partial self-portrait of the Mahatma emerges from the whole.

Krishna, Gopal. "The Development of the Indian National Congress as a Mass Organization, 1918–1923," *Journal of Asian Studies,* XXV, no. 3 (May 1966), 413–30. An important article on the transformation of the Congress from a relatively small, elite organization into a much wider, deeper one in the early Gandhian years.

Low, D.A. (ed.). *Soundings in Modern South Asian History.* London: Weidenfeld and Nicolson, 1968. A diverse collection of articles dealing with Indian society and politics in the nineteenth and twentieth centuries. Several valuable articles deal with the

136

Home Rule Leagues and the development of noncooperation in the period 1915 to 1922.

Discussion Topics and Questions

1. Analyze the factors contributing to the successful rise of Mahatma Gandhi in Indian politics.
2. How is the method and philosophy of satyagraha related to Indian traditions?
3. Analyze the response of the Government of India to the noncooperation movement?
4. Analyze Hindu-Muslim relations in period 1915–1928.

XIV. THE GROWTH OF THE LEFT AND STRAINS IN INDIAN POLITICS

A. Influx of leftist ideas and organizers after Russian Revolution
   1. Little impact of socialist ideas before end of World War I
   2. Nationalist exiles outside India
      a. Touched by socialist, communist currents
      b. Contacts with Third Communist International from 1919
         1) Communists choose M.N. Roy, former Bengal revolutionary, as chief ideologue, organizer for India
         2) Other Indians compete with Roy for communist support
      c. Roy's work, 1919 to 1925
         1) Sends funds, agents to organize communist cells
         2) Writes *India in Transition,* 1922; fullest Marxist analysis of Indian society, nationalism to that time
         3) Communist propaganda smuggled into India
         4) Advance of communism in India greatly overestimated by Roy, other exiles
   3. Small communist groups formed Bombay, Calcutta, elsewhere
      a. Number and influence limited in 1920s
      b. Government gives prominence to communists by arrests, trials; Cawnpore (1924) and Meerut (1929) Conspiracy Cases
   4. Jawaharlal Nehru, Tagore visit Soviet Union
      a. Both write favorable accounts

137

        b. Nehru imbues nationalist ideas with socialist ideology, critique of capitalism, imperialism

    5. Communist critiques of Gandhi

        a. Ambivalence about supporting mass movement he commands

        b. Roy sees Gandhi as tool of reactionary cultural and bourgeois interests

B. Strains in Indian politics

  1. Regional

    a. Bengal, Maharashtra: strong anti-Gandhi feeling

      1) Battlegrounds of Swarajists vs. No-Changers, 1920s

      2) Supply ideological critiques of Gandhi

      3) Supply leaders for Hindu Mahasabha, Forward Bloc, both very critical of Gandhi from different viewpoints

    b. Madras Presidency: Andhra movement against Tamil domination

  2. Communal and ethnic (see XV on Muslims)

    a. Justice Party in Madras based on non-Brahman support

      1) Opposes Brahman domination within Madras Congress

      2) Wants communal representation

      3) In turn draws fire of Madras untouchables

    b. Untouchables

      1) Gandhi calls them "Harijans" (children of God) and works for uplift, end of their exclusion from Hindu society

      2) Work of Dr. B.R. Ambedkar

        a) Educated, talented untouchable suffers from discrimination

        b) Becomes leading spokesman for untouchables, 1930s on

      3) Government of India Communal Award, 1932

        a) Communal representation (reserved seats and separate electorates) for untouchables

        b) Gandhi's fast against such separation of untouchables

        c) Government and Ambedkar finally yield

        d) Reserved seats with joint electorates for untouchables agreed upon

  3. Ideological and class (see below, Left, sections C., D.)

C. Congress leftists and the Congress Socialist Party (C.S.P.)

  1. Spread of socialist ideas, programs in Congress

    a. Activity of young, militant Congressmen, Jawaharlal Nehru and Subhas Chandra Bose

    b. Push Congress program leftward demanding stress on achievement of social and economic equality

    c. Efforts in 1928–1931 to gain Congress recognition of independence demand and socialist program

    d. Independence demand, some socialist goals adopted by Karachi Declaration of Congress, 1931

  2. Leftists try organizing workers and peasants in trade unions, Kisan Sabhas

  3. Congress Socialist Party formed, early 1930s, by Jayaprakash Narayan, M.R. Masani, R. Lohia, Asoka Mehta, Acharya Narendra Dev, others

    a. Work within Congress for socialist program

    b. Unsuccessful at recruiting Nehru, Bose, who link Gandhian High Command and leftists in Congress

  4. Nehru Congress Secretary, then Congress President, 1936, 1937

    a. Puts C.S.P. men on Working Committee

    b. Prevents split between left and right in Congress

  5. Subhas Bose, Congress President, 1938

    a. Gandhi put Bose in to tame him

    b. Bose works with Gandhian leaders during 1938

D. Congress crisis and the divided left

  1. Bose's challenge

    a. Runs for Congress president against Gandhian candidate, 1939

    b. Wins, but limited under Pant Resolution passed by Tripuri Congress

    c. Left divided at Tripuri and subsequently

    d. Bose, feeling lack of solid support, resigns

  2. Gandhians regain complete control of Working Committee

  3. Communists purged from C.S.P.

    a. C.S.P. moves closer to Gandhi

    b. C.S.P. disbands during World War II

  4. Bose forms Forward Bloc

    a. Attempt at leftist unity but becomes another splinter group

    b. Suspended from Congress organization

  5. Communists work within Congress following United Front line during 1930s

    a. Imperialist War, 1939–1941: Communists oppose war effort

    b. People's War, 1941–1945: once Soviet Union fighting with Allies, Indian communists support war effort

c. As consequence of war work views, communists purged from Congress

Reading Assignments

Brecher, *Nehru,* chapters V, X
Sources of Indian Tradition, 887–924; paperback, 335–72

Optional Assignment

Overstreet, Gene D., and Marshall Windmiller. *Communism in India.* Berkeley: University of California, 1959. The best general history of the Indian Communist Party written to date. Although it does not deal very well with the social context and background of the party's leadership and operations, it uses many inaccessible sources and is widely read even by the party faithful.

Additional Readings

Bose, Subhas Chandra. *The Indian Struggle, 1920–1942.* Calcutta: Asia Publishing House, 1964. An account of the nationalist movement by an important participant in it. The writer criticizes the inadequacies of Gandhi and the Congress High Command and advocates a more militant, socialist line.

Fanon, Frantz, *The Wretched of the Earth.* New York: Grove Press paperback, 1963. Deeply felt, impassioned indictment of colonialism by a psychiatrist who became involved in the struggle of the Algerians for independence from the French. He stresses the cathartic value of violence for the oppressed. His views may be compared to those of some Indian revolutionaries and communists who would have agreed with him.

Irschick, Eugene F. *Politics and Social Conflict in South India. The Non-Brahman Movement and Tamil Separatism 1916–1929.* Berkeley: University of California Press, 1969. A valuable historical analysis.

Narayan, Jaya Prakash. *Towards Struggle.* Bombay: Padma Publications, 1946. Autobiographical notes and political analyses by a founder of the Congress Socialist Party. The author was a leader of the violent uprising in 1942, a leading socialist after independence, and later a follower of Vinoba Bhave's nonviolent, nonpolitical Gandhian movement.

Nehru, Jawaharlal. *Toward Freedom.* Boston: Beacon Press, 1958. The autobiography of an important Congress leader who became India's prime minister and a world figure. It comes up to 1935 and gives a passionate and vivid account of the resurgence of the Congress in the 1920s and 1930s and of the author's relationship to Gandhi.

Roy, M.N. *India in Transition.* Geneva: J.B. Target, 1922. The first systematic Marxist analysis of the nationalist movement in India by a Bengal revolutionary who became the founder of the Indian Communist Party. This book was banned in India and was smuggled in during the nationalist period.

Rusch, Thomas A., "Role of the Congress Socialist Party in the Indian National Congress, 1931–1942." Ph.D. thesis, University of Chicago, 1955. The best analysis of the Congress socialists, based on wide research and interviews conducted in India in the 1950s.

Spratt, Philip. *Blowing Up India.* Calcutta: Prachi Prakshan, 1955. A subtle and interesting autobiography of an Englishman who was sent to India in the 1920s by the Third Communist International to help organize the Indian Communist Party and the trade union movement in India.

Discussion Topics and Questions

1. How might one explain the delayed influence of socialist ideas in India, as compared to Europe?
2. Discuss the reasons for the internecine struggle between leftists in India from the 1920s to the present.
3. Why was India a fertile ground for the spread of socialist ideas? Evaluate the successes and failures of socialist and communist political groups in India before 1947.
4. Why wasn't Subhas Bose more successful in uniting the left behind him in 1939? In what ways is 1939 a turning point in the history of the left in India?
5. Analyze the political and personal relationships between Jawaharlal Nehru, Subhas Bose, and Mahatma Gandhi.
6. Analyze the gaps between Congress ideology and Congress accomplishment up to 1947.

XV. THE DEVELOPMENT OF MUSLIM POLITICS

A. Nineteenth-century background (see VI)
   1. Fundamentalist movements: Wahabi and Fara-idi
   2. Revivalism: Deoband school
      a. Cultural, religious movement for freedom from British in United Provinces

      b. Madrassah, founded 1867, helps train Muslims in tradi-
tional education; also popularize Urdu

      c. Graduates enter journalism, teaching, business; others
preachers, active ulamas

   3. Modernism: Sir Syed Ahmad Khan and Aligarh school

      a. Modern interpretation of Islam

      b. Western and Islamic learning

      c. Loyalist political position

B. Muslim League, founded 1906

   1. Program to protect, further interests of Muslims

   2. Irregular and limited meetings well into 1930s

C. Anti-loyalist trends, early twentieth century

   1. Some Aligarh graduates and Professor Shibli Nu'mani question loyalism

   2. Muhammad Ali (1879–1930)

      a. Founds *Comrade,* one of most sophisticated, intelligent
papers in India before World War I

      b. Criticism of communal patriots' narrowness

         1) Hindus and Muslims must widen vision

         2) Communal individualities must be recognized

      c. Defense of Turkish Khilafat (as supreme Muslim religious
authority) while British fighting Turks, World War I

      d. Imprisoned by government during wartime

   3. Maulana Abul Kalam Azad (1888–1958)

      a. Born Mecca, thorough Islamic education

      b. Strong defense of Khilafat in Urdu paper, *al-Hilāl*

      c. Member of religious reform group

      d. Work in Khilafat movement and Congress involvement

   4. Britain fights Turkey, World War I

      a. Impact on Indian Muslims with strong ties to Khilafat

      b. Emotional Islamic feeling against oppressive foreigners in
Muslim India and Middle East

      c. Maulana Ubaidullah Sindhi sets up Provisional Govern-
ment in Afghanistan during war and some Indian Muslims
cross border

D. Cultural trends

   1. Hindi versus Urdu controversy from late nineteenth century

      a. Muslims feel Raj on Hindi side

      b. Adds to anti-governmental feeling

      c. Muslim leaders Azad, Muhammad Ali foster writing in
Urdu

   2. Jam'iyyat-al-'Ulama' founded 1919

a. Strong Deoband influence
b. Distrust of Westernized Muslims
c. Loyalty to Islam and India
d. Cooperation with Congress
3. Muhammad Iqbal (1876–1938)
a. Leading Muslim poet and philosopher in twentieth-century India
b. Writes poetry, prose in Urdu and Persian; appeal to educated
c. Emphasizes benefits of Islamic teachings for solving modern dilemmas
d. Evils of European nationalism
e. Multinational concept of Pan-Islam
E. Honeymoon period of Hindu-Muslim relations, 1916 to 1923
1. Lucknow Pact (see XIII above)
2. Khilafat agitation part of nationwide Noncooperation
a. Hindus and Muslims work together organizationally
b. Maulana Azad, Muhammad and Shakat Ali leaders
c. Muslim lawyer politicians, e.g., Mohammad Ali Jinnah, Fazlul Huq, oppose Noncooperation
F. The widening gulf and attempts to bridge it
1. Moplah riots in South: communal and economic antagonisms, mid-1920s
2. Riots in Bengal, elsewhere, from end of World War I
3. Bengal Pact and its demise
a. C.R. Das attempts communal unity by giving Muslims concessions, especially in government jobs in Calcutta Corporation which nationalists control or will control with further constitutional advances
b. Pact not accepted by Indian National Congress and dies
4. All-Parties Conference, 1928: Nehru Report unacceptable to many Muslims
5. Jinnah (1876–1948), moving to Muslim League leadership, lists fourteen Points on which Muslims want agreement, 1928; no bargain made
6. Some Muslims support Congress
a. Frontier Red shirts led by Abdul Ghaffar Khan
b. Jam'iyyat-al-'Ulama'
c. A few prominent figures, e.g., Azad, Zakar Hussain
7. Jinnah leaves scene in early 1930s
8. Muslim League lags in mobilizing support but claims to speak for all Muslims

Reading Assignments

Brown, *United States and India and Pakistan,* chapter 7
Sources of Indian Tradition, 747–81, 827–40; paperback, 195–229,
275–88

Optional Assignment

Sayeed, Khalid Bin. *Pakistan, The Formative Phase.* Second edition.
London: Oxford University Press, 1968. The best work written to
date on the development of the Muslim League and the Pakistan
movement. It deals in most detail with the period 1940 to 1948
and contains a shrewd assessment of Jinnah.

Additional Readings

Ahmad, Aziz. *Islamic Modernism in India and Pakistan 1857–1964.*
London: Oxford University Press, 1967. A useful cultural history
tracing modernistic and traditional movements.
Faruqi, Ziya-ul-Hasan. *The Deoband School and the Demand for
Pakistan.* Bombay: Asia Publishing House, 1963. An invaluable
account of a traditionalist anti-British movement which sided
with the Congress against the Muslim League.
Gopal, Ram. *The Indian Muslims, A Political History.* Bombay:
Asia Publishing House, 1959. A general and useful history of
Muslim politics written by a Hindu who is not entirely sympa-
thetic to Muslim grievances and separatism.
Khan, Aga. *Memoirs, World Enough and Time.* London: Cassell,
1954. Valuable memoirs of a world figure who lobbied for the
Muslim League in London during the early years of its existence.
The author, of course, inflates his own role.
Muhammad Ali, Chaudhri. *The Emergence of Pakistan.* New York:
Columbia University Press, 1967. Inside account of the Pakistan
movement by a politician who later became Finance Minister
and Prime Minister of independent Pakistan. He deals mostly
with the 1940s.
Saiyid, M.H. *Mohammad Ali Jinnah.* Second edition. Lahore: Sh.
Muhammad Ashraf, 1962. One of the biographies of Jinnah
which contains some useful information but, like the others, is
marred by excessive idolization of the subject. A first-rate biography of Jinnah has yet to be written.

Discussion Topics and Questions

1. Have Hindus and Muslims always been "two nations," as many
Muslims have claimed?

2. Describe the social and economic bases of Muslim political organizations.
3. Was the movement towards partition inevitable in terms of developments to 1925? 1930? 1937?
4. Discuss the Congress and government views of the Muslim League.
5. How justifiable were Muslim fears about living in a Hindu-dominated free India?

XVI. TO PARTITION AND INDEPENDENCE

A. Questions about the partition
  1. Wide variation in dating point from which partition inevitable
    a. Most Muslim writers trace developments back to Sir Syed Ahmad Khan
    b. Counterargument: even in early 1940s was still possible to preserve Indian unity
  2. Assessing responsibility
    a. Number of strong personalities with crucial roles
    b. Tendency to blame others in partisan accounts
    c. Need inclusive historical view
  3. Problems in evaluating two-nation and one-nation theories
    a. Both based on evaluation of historical developments
    b. Both advocated, although solid historical studies of Hindu-Muslim relations still needed for such evaluations
B. Government of India Act, 1935, and its consequences
  1. Provisions: provincial autonomy and arrangements for states' participation at the center
  2. Elections held, 1936–1937
    a. Congress does well: wins 714 of 1585 total seats in provincial elections: most in general or Hindu constituencies
    b. Muslim League wins 109 of 485 Muslim seats
  3. After controversy with government about terms of office acceptance, Congress takes office in seven of eleven provinces
    a. Congress rule in Madras, Bombay, United Provinces, Central Provinces, Bihar, North West Frontier Province, Assam (in coalition)
    b. Except in Assam, Congressmen prevented from coalition attempts even if local Congress wants it; e.g., Bengal

4. Non-Congress governments
   a. Muslim coalition led by Fazlul Huq in Bengal
      1) Unstable alliance between Huq's Krishak Praja Party and League
      2) Huq later realigns ministry with support of Congress faction, 1941–1943
   b. Unionist government in Punjab led by Sikander Hyat Khan; includes Hindus, Muslims, Sikhs
   c. Muslim-dominated government or official control, Sind, Orissa
5. United Provinces ministry question and Muslim fears
   a. Election alliance between League and Congress in United Provinces
   b. After big Congress victory, Congress insists all ministers be Congress members
      1) Effectively excludes League participation
      2) League fears similar cases will arise in free India, and Muslims will not have protections
6. Congress attempts organizing of Muslim masses to undercut League
   a. Organizing is relatively unsuccessful
   b. Spurs League on to do its own organizing of Muslim masses
7. League lists atrocities under Congress rule
   a. Many seem invented
   b. Propaganda impact
C. Pakistan movement
   1. Jinnah builds League support
      a. Mass contact program successful, 1937 to 1946
      b. Calls for protection of Muslim cultural, religious, economic, political, social interests
   2. Iqbal's notion of autonomous Islamic state in northwest part of India formulated in 1930
   3. Muslim students at Cambridge suggest name "Pakistan" in 1930s
   4. League adopts "Pakistan Resolution," 1940, calling for independent Islamic states in Muslim-majority areas
   5. Unclear how determined League is on this course early 1940s
D. World War II and Indian politics
   1. Government of India declares war, 1939, and Congress ministries resign because not consulted

146

    a. Congress favors Allies but wants concessions for support
    b. Resignations open way for other political groups to advance
  2. Support of government war efforts
    a. League gives cautious support and wants concessions
    b. Communists and M.N. Roy followers support government and get financial aid
    c. Liberals work with government
  3. Cripps Mission, 1942
    a. Dominion status offered after war
    b. Congress declines offer; wants greater powers immediately
  4. Congress moves to noncooperation, 1942
    a. "Quit India" movement with limited individual noncooperation led by Gandhi
    b. Rebellion in some places led by Congress socialists, especially Jayaprakash Narayan
    c. Congress leaders imprisoned for duration of war
  5. Subhas Bose and the Indian National Army (I.N.A.)
    a. Bose escapes house arrest, 1941
    b. Works with Germans and Indian prisoners in Europe, 1941–1943
    c. Bose to Southeast Asia, 1943
      1) Takes command; Indian National Army mainly prisoners-of-war
      2) Forms Provincial Government of Azad Hind (Free India)
      3) I.N.A. fights in Burma with Japanese
      4) Pushed back, Bose dies in crash, 1945
E. Post-war elections and negotiations deadlocked
  1. Cabinet Mission
    a. Cripps, Pethick-Lawrence come, 1946, representing new Labour Government
    b. League-Congress division prevents agreement
  2. 1946 elections: League wins great majority of Muslim seats, demonstrating its support
  3. Federation plans discussed
  4. Interim government formed
    a. Nehru is Prime Minister and Congress holds most top posts
    b. League boycotts, then joins
      1) Demands important posts

      2) Liaquat Ali Khan of League as Finance Minister
      3) Deadlocks in governing make partition idea more palatable
  5. League turns to direct action, 1946
    a. Great Calcutta Killing and other serious communal riots follow
    b. Threat of civil war hangs heavy
F. Mountbatten and the partition
  1. British Government announcements
    a. Will pull out in 1948
    b. Mountbatten appointed Viceroy to handle transfer of power
  2. Mountbatten decides must be partition
    a. Persuades Nehru, Sardar Patel to accept idea for Congress
    b. Fearing difficulties of weak federal scheme, they accept
    c. Gandhi does not like partition, but no longer deciding voice in Congress
  3. Government sets date of August 15, 1947 for British exit
    a. Radcliffe commission draws up boundaries of two nations
    b. Communities vote and Pakistan, composed of areas in northwest and northeast India, approved by Muslim voters
  4. Gandhi helps quell communal violence, Bengal, Delhi area
  5. Mountbatten works to have several hundred semi-independent Indian states accede to one or the other of the two new nations
  6. Around partition date much violence and movement
    a. Great population transfers by fearful Hindus and Muslims in Bengal, by Hindus, Muslims, and Sikhs in Punjab
    b. Serious riots and slaughter of untold thousands, especially in Punjab
    c. Gandhi works for calm in Delhi area
  7. Deaths of Gandhi and Jinnah
    a. Gandhi: assassinated in January 1948 by Hindu fanatic who believed him too pro-Muslim
    b. In same year, Jinnah dies: fathers of the two new nations dead within a year of independence

Reading Assignments

Brecher, *Nehru,* chapters XI–XIV
Brown, *United States and India and Pakistan,* chapters 6, 8
Woodruff, *Men Who Ruled India,* volume II, part II, chapters IV–VIII

Optional Assignment

Moon, Penderel. *Divide and Quit.* London: Chatto and Windus, 1961. The most insightful and most interesting book written on the partition. The author was a high-ranking civil servant who witnessed the partition and its gruesome aftermath in Bahawalpur State and the Punjab. In his conclusions he critically assesses the responsibilities of Gandhi, Jinnah, and the British.

Additional Readings

Emerson, Rupert. *From Empire to Nation.* Cambridge: Harvard University Press, 1960 and paperback. A general account of the process of decolonization and the drive for self-determination by the peoples of Asia and Africa following World War II.

Hodson, H.V. *The Great Divide: Britain, India, Pakistan.* London: Hutchinson, 1969. A recent important account of the partition by a writer who had access to Lord Mountbattan's papers.

Menon, V.P. *The Transfer of Power In India.* Princeton: Princeton University Press, 1957. Detailed account of the partition negotiations by an official who served as constitutional adviser and link man between the Viceroy and the Congress; critical of Muslim League intransigence.

Singh, Khushwant. *Mano Majra.* (Also published as *Train to Pakistan.*) New York: Grove Press, 1950. Novel by a Sikh writer about the impact of the partition on the peoples of the Punjab.

Tuker, Francis. *While Memory Serves.* London: Cassell, 1950. Vivid, gory account of the last few years of the British Raj as seen by the commanding officer of the Eastern Command. He describes the Bengali politicians at work for and against the partition, Gandhi's days in Calcutta, and the Great Calcutta Killing.

Wallbank, T. Walter (ed.). *The Partition of India.* Boston: Heath paperback, 1966. A useful collection of writings about the partition by some of the Hindus, Muslims, and British involved and by a number of outside analysts.

Discussion Topics and Questions

1. When did the partition become inevitable: what were the crucial periods, steps, and events leading to the partition?
2. Why did the British decide to quit India?
3. What part did personality factors, particularly those of Jinnah, Gandhi, Nehru, and Mountbatten, play in shaping the partition?

4. Did the partition make sense economically?
5. What groups and leaders opposed the partition and why?

XVII. INDIA AND PAKISTAN: INTEGRATION OF THE
STATES AND MUTUAL RELATIONS

A. Problems of the states
   1. Significance for India and Pakistan
      a. Represent about one-third of total area of India and Pakistan
      b. More than 500, greatly varying in size, development
      c. Many favor independence as British leave
   2. Accession
      a. Pressed by Mountbatten most accede to either India or Pakistan before independence
      b. Give up even limited autonomy enjoyed under British Raj
      c. Receive annual privy purses
   3. Important states which hesitate
      a. Hyderabad: huge state in center of south India
         1) Muslim ruler, Hindu majority population
         2) Determined Muslim group desiring ties to Pakistan
         3) Lengthy negotiations involving V.P. Menon, Patel, Mountbatten, Nizam of Hyderabad, other officials, 1947–1948
         4) Stories of Nizam's weapons purchases, negotiations with Pakistan
         5) Upheaval in state set off by Muslim Razakars, communists
         6) September 1948, Indian troops move in and accession follows
      b. Kashmir
         1) Hindu ruler, Muslim majority population
         2) Of great importance strategically to India, Pakistan; borders China
         3) Maharaja hesitates on accession to either India or Pakistan
         4) Invasion of frontier tribesmen, October 1947
         5) India agrees to aid if Maharaja accedes; he agrees
         6) Indian troops move in; provisional ceasefire line set

7) Numerous attempts by U.N. to settle matter unsuccessful
8) India holds more desirable parts; prefers status quo
9) Pakistan insists Muslims forced to live under Hindu Raj and tires to unsettle status quo
10) Kashmir question major barrier to better Indo-Pakistani relations
B. Course of Indo-Pakistani relations
   1. Both countries unhappy about division of territory and resources
      a. Pakistan feels Mountbatten influenced Radcliffe border settlement in India's favor
      b. Pakistan feels she got less of resources, matériel
         1) India stalls on transfer of currency reserves
         2) Gandhi's fast forces Patel to carry agreement through
      c. Continuing problem of water resources
         1) Necessitates cooperation between two countries
         2) Settlement worked out in Punjab; Indus Waters Treaty signed 1960 with World Bank aid
         3) Unresolved question of Ganges water division in Bengal
   2. Minorities problem
      a. Although great numbers move, many Muslims remain in India, considerable number of Hindus remain in East Pakistan
      b. Minorities feel like second-class citizens
      c. Each country says it treats them well and blames other
      d. Continuing trickle across borders, especially in east
      e. Occasional communal riots; minorities suffer
   3. Declining trade between two countries and costly rivalries, e.g., jute production
   4. Border war, 1965
      a. Fought to standstill, West Pakistan, western India
      b. Tashkent Agreement follows
      c. Basic bitterness and distrust remains

Reading Assignments

Brecher, *Nehru,* chapter XV
Brown, *United States and India and Pakistan,* chapters 9, 10

Additional Readings

Choudhuiy, G.W. *Pakistan's Relations with India 1947–1966.* New York: Praeger, 1968. An account of the embittered relations between India and Pakistan written from the Pakistani point of view by an academic who has become a government official.

Gupta, Sisir. *India and Regional Integration in Asia*. New York: Asia Publishing House, 1964. A general account of India's foreign policy and of India's problems in the South Asia region, principally with Pakistan. Written by an Indian with a long interest in Pakistani affairs.

Korbel, Josef. *Danger in Kashmir*. Revised edition. Princeton University Press paperback, 1966. One of the better analyses of the Kashmir problem, written originally in the 1950s. A chapter was added in the mid-1960s bringing the account up to date.

Menon, V.P. *The Story of the Integration of the Indian States*. Bombay: Orient Longmans, 1956. A detailed, firsthand account of the integration of more than 500 former princely states into the Republic of India, written by a crucial figure in the operation who served as Secretary to the Ministry of States.

Wilcox Wayne A. *Pakistan: The Consolidation of a Nation*. New York: Columbia University Press, 1963. Valuable account of the integration of former princely states into Pakistan. Complements the volume by Menon on this process in India.

Also see general works on Indian and Pakistani foreign policy cited in XVIII.

Discussion Topics and Questions

1. Discuss the moments at which Indian-Pakistan relations improved and why no further progress towards harmonious relations was made.
2. Discuss the role of the United Nations and outside powers in the attempts at rapprochement between India and Pakistan.
3. Discuss the economic consequences of the partition for India and Pakistan.
4. Discuss Indian rule in Kashmir and the course of internal Kashmiri politics since 1947.
5. Discuss the possibilities for improved relations between India and Pakistan. What issues must be resolved first? What are the secondary issues?

XVIII. INDIA AND PAKISTAN IN THE WORLD
COMMUNITY

A. Pre-independence trends
  1. Interests of Indian nationalists in other freedom struggles against Western rule, e.g., Asian, African countries, Ireland
  2. Nehru's long-standing interest in foreign affairs, anti-imperialism
  3. Another Indian tradition represented by Subhas Bose: foreign affairs shaped by hard self-interest
  4. Muslim interest in the wider Muslim world
    a. Heightened at time of Khilafat agitation
    b. Continuing interest in Pan-Islam
B. India: trying to play a world role
  1. Nehru designs policy of positive neutrality, nonalignment
    a. Seeks activist role in settling important conflicts
    b. Takes neutral stand on issues, but generally more critical of Western than of Communist powers
    c. Tries to influence other former colonies to adopt this line
    d. Tries to bring Third World states together
    e. Criticizes anticommunist pacts, e.g., SEATO
  2. Early successes
    a. Korean conflict
      1) India actively seeks to mediate
      2) India on Neutral Nations Repatriation Commission; its tasks successfully completed
      3) Hard feelings on both sides
    b. Bandung Conference, April 1955
      1) Nehru at center stage
      2) Sino-Indian relations appear warm
      3) "Pansheela" or Five Principles of Peaceful Coexistence agreed to by India, China
    c. India active at Geneva Conference on Indochina, 1954
    d. India chosen head of International Control Commission (I.C.C.) for Indochina
      1) A few early successes
      2) I.C.C. becomes virtually impotent after U.S., South Vietnam prevent 1956 elections
      3) Indian aim of neutralization of Laos, Cambodia, Vietnam temporarily effective in Laos, Cambodia
      4) India critical of U.S. involvement; would like to help end war

3. Nonaligned but recipient of large amounts of aid
    a. India's middle course, size and importance allow her to work for, receive aid from both Western powers and Communist bloc
    b. Food and economic aid from the U.S.
        1) Period 1951–1965, about $6 billion in aid
        2) U.S. hesitation to support large projects in public sector (e.g., Bokaro)
        3) Some military aid after Chinese border clash
    c. Considerable aid from U.S.S.R.
        1) Willingness to support large projects in public sector
        2) Support of Bokaro Steel Plant when U.S. stalls, early 1960s
    d. Problem of strings attached to foreign aid
        1) India resistant to such influences
        2) Some evidence of implicit vetos on some Indian moves by major-aid-givers (e.g., Indian hesitation to upgrade consulate in Hanoi)
4. Deterioration of Sino-Indian relations
    a. Honeymoon period in 1950s
    b. India acquiesces in Tibetan take-over by China
    c. Conflicting border claims become live issue from late 1950s
    d. Hostilities break out on frontier, 1962
    e. India secures aid from U.S., Britain
    f. Chinese do not press military advantage
    g. Stalemate on border claims and poor Sino-Indian relations
5. Nuclear power question
    a. India has capacity to build atomic weapons
    b. Uses foreign assistance to build atomic plants for peaceful ends
    c. Great debate on whether India should build bomb
C. Pakistan: search for support and allies
    1. As smaller state in area, Pakistan looks for support
        a. Fear of Indian take-over
        b. Overtures to Islamic world bear few fruits
    2. Ties to the U.S.
        a. U.S. looking for anticommunist allies, 1950s
        b. Pakistan looking for economic aid and aid against Indian threat
        c. Pakistan joins SEATO, 1954, CENTO, 1955

d. Pakistan receives large amounts U.S. economic, military aid
  1) From 1954–1960, Pakistan receives $1.5 billion in military aid
  2) 1956–1965, about $3 billion in economic aid
3. Shifts from late 1950s
  a. Sino-Indian conflict makes Pakistan uncertain about U.S. tie
  b. Some officials see advantages of nonaligned position
  c. Under Ayub Khan regime, and especially with Bhutto as foreign minister, Pakistan improves relations with communists
    1) Relations with Soviet Union improved
    2) Border settlement with China signed, 1963
  d. Pakistan very critical of U.S. involvement in Vietnam

Reading Assignments

Brecher, *Nehru,* chapter XIX
Brown, *United States and India and Pakistan,* chapters 15, 16

Optional Assignments

Palmer, Norman D. *South Asia and U.S. Policy.* Boston: Houghton Mifflin paperback, 1966. A general and detailed account of the relations of India and Pakistan to the United States. The author explores foreign aid programs, problems of defense and security, and the whole range of foreign policy problems of India and Pakistan.

Sayeed, K.B. *The Political System of Pakistan.* Boston: Houghton Mifflin paperback, 1967. One of the finest general books on contemporary Pakistani politics, containing a valuable chapter on Pakistan's foreign policy.

Additional Readings

Bhutto, Zulfikar Ali. *The Myth of Independence.* London: Oxford University Press, 1969. An impassioned and opinionated assessment of Pakistan's foreign policy dilemmas by her former Foreign Minister. He suggests that small powers like Pakistan play off one large power against another. Bhutto also details the ways in which the United States has been trying to impose its will on South Asia.

Brecher, Michael. *The New States of Asia.* London: Oxford University Press paperback, 1963. A comparative study of the problems of the new nations of Asia. One essay gives a fine exposition of India's policy of positive neutrality.

Harrison, Selig. "India, Pakistan and the United States," *New Republic,* August 10, August 24, September 7, 1960. A very important series of articles detailing the machinations behind the making of security arrangements between Pakistan and the United States in the early 1950s. India's antipathy to Pakistan's entry into SEATO and to Pakistan's receipt of American arms is explained. The author was America's foremost journalist in India for many years.

Power, Paul. F. (ed.). *India's Nonalignment Policy.* Boston: Heath paperback, 1967. A collection of articles favoring, explaining, and criticizing India's general foreign policy position.

SarDesai, D. R. *Indian Foreign Policy in Cambodia, Laos, and Vietnam, 1947–1964.* Berkeley: University of California Press, 1968. Systematic and detailed account of India's relation to the conflicts in Indochina over the past twenty-five years.

Discussion Topics and Questions

1. What factors have restricted India's role as a positive neutral more severely in the 1960s than in the 1950s?
2. Why did the Pakistani government move towards a more non-aligned position?
3. What stakes does the U.S. have in South Asia? The U.S.S.R.? China?
4. Discuss the views of Pakistan and India and public opinion in these two countries on the war in Indochina.
5. Discuss the positive and negative consequences of foreign aid to India and Pakistan.

XIX. PROBLEMS OF INDEPENDENCE FOR INDIA AND PAKISTAN: SOCIAL AND ECONOMIC

A. India
   1. Economic planning and development
      a. Plans and implementation
         1) Five-year plans, 1951–1956, 1956–1961, 1961–1966, bring mixed results

2) Early stress on heavy industry following Soviet example
3) Food production lag brings more attention to agriculture
4) Village and block development schemes
   a) Variety of schemes for intensive development tried
   b) Benefits often to most important families in villages
   c) Lack of adequate means of checking plan implementation
b. Industrialization and nationalization
  1) Public sector efforts in transport, communications, steel, atomic energy
  2) Several large industrial-commercial groups well protected, encouraged under Congress rule; e.g., Tata and Birla groups
  3) Congress program calls for nationalization: Mrs. Gandhi moves to nationalize foreign banks
c. Tax collection difficulties hamper government
d. Income trend studies show economic disparities not decreasing
e. On the land
  1) Redistribution legislation
   a) 1950 Zamindari Abolition Act in United Provinces (and similarly other states)
   b) 1955 survey shows 10 percent own 50 percent of land
   c) Legislation helps end era of great absentee landlords
  2) Forced labor decreasing, but landless labor increasing
  3) Bhoodan or land gift movement of Vinoba Bhave
   a) Voluntary gifts requested in effort to redistribute land and help poor
   b) In practice, poor land given and benefits limited
  4) Green Revolution in food grains
   a) Use of better seeds and techniques
   b) Agricultural production increased, especially in Punjab
   c) Too early to judge impact
2. Social and cultural problems
a. Demography and population control
  1) Immediately after independence not taken seriously enough
  2) Last few years greater efforts at population control
  3) Population growth down very slightly; vast effort needed to make adequate impact

b. Language questions
  1) States reorganization: pressures for linguistic states acceded to and state boundaries made more congruent with language areas
    a) Bombay split into Maharashtra and Gujerat, 1960
    b) Punjab split into Punjabi Suba and Haryana, 1966
  2) Spread of regional languages as media of instruction at all levels
  3) National language question
    a) Hindi officially the national language
    b) *De facto* use of English for center–state purposes because of resistance to Hindi, especially in south
    c) Involves economic issues, e.g., recruitment for services
    d) Riots in south India, 1965, when Hindi imposed
c. Scheduled castes and tribes
  1) Government efforts to aid through reserved places in legislatures, services, educational institutions
  2) Reservation of seats (with joint constituencies) helps muffle protest as well as serve interests of people
  3) Vocal criticisms demanding redistribution of benefits to economically deprived rather than present system of reservations
  4) Untouchables still suffer grave problems of acceptance by caste society
d. Unrest of peasants, workers, students
  1) Peasants encouraged to take land from large holders
  2) Considerable amount of sporadic rural violence
  3) Workers use new technique of "gheraos," surrounding opponent, to gain immediate redress of grievances
  4) Students long active in politics
  5) Student unrest against political and administrative authorities coupled with considerable unemployment of educated
  6) Prospect of continuing and growing unrest
B. Pakistan
  1. Economic planning and development
    a. Independence gives Muslims more opportunity to develop business, commerce, professions
    b. Five-year plans, 1955–1960, 1960–1965, 1965–1970
      1) Government industrial and power corporations
      2) Government control by checking flow of necessary imports for private enterprise

     c. 1947–1959: urban economy growing fast, but industrial base small

     d. Changes under new regime after 1959
        1) Some of previous controls abandoned
        2) Economic growth rate up as G.N.P. climbs rapidly
        3) Foreign aid gives needed boost
        4) Industrial, urban sector benefits most
        5) Widened economic inequality though rapid growth
        6) Rising expectations and rising frustration, especially in East Pakistan and among educated
        7) Industrial sector still small in absolute figures: 9 percent of national product in mid-1960s

     e. On the land
        1) 1947–1959: agricultural stagnation
        2) 1959 on: agriculture doing better, but agriculturalists benefiting least from economic growth

2. Social and cultural problems
     a. Regional strains (see XX below)
        1) Widespread feeling against central government in East Pakistan
           a) Language riots, 1952
           b) West Pakistanis still dominate army, business, though East Pakistanis coming to parity in services
           c) 1971 crisis (see XX below)
        2) In West Pakistan, Sind feelings against Punjabi domination

     b. Questions of Islamic and Pakistani identity
        1) Country based on religious division of British India
        2) Some doubts by more secular Muslims about Islam as basis for a modern nation

Reading Assignments

Brecher, *Nehru,* chapter XVIII
Brown, *United States and India and Pakistan,* chapters 13, 14

Optional Assignments

Nair, Kusum. *Blossoms in the Dust. The Human Factor in Indian Development.* New York: Praeger, 1961. A vivid account of problems of agricultural and social development in rural India. The author traveled around the country from province to province and village to village talking to peasants, landlords, government officials, and landless laborers. She has been criticized for being pessimistic, but her work is widely read.

Singer, Milton, and Bernard S. Cohn. *Structure and Change in Indian Society*. Chicago: Aldine, 1968. An important collection of essays by anthropologists of South Asia confronting substantive and theoretical problems of social structure, caste, politics, language, family, and social change.

Additional Readings

Bailey, F.G. *Tribe, Caste and Nation*. Bombay: Oxford University Press, 1960. *Caste and the Economic Frontier*. Manchester: Manchester University Press, 1957. Pathbreaking studies by one of the premier anthropologists of India focusing on a small area in Orissa. The author tries to analyze the interactions and changes in three systems: the tribal system of the Konds; Oriya society, based upon caste; and the modern economic, political, and administrative systems impinging upon the local area.

Bettelheim, Charles. *India Independent*. New York: Monthly Review Press, 1968. A general analysis of India's political economy by a scholar with a Marxist bent. Much more critical than American accounts of the role of foreign capital in Indian development.

Epstein, T. Scarlett. *Economic Development and Social Change in South India*. Manchester: Manchester University Press, 1962. A valuable study focusing on related economic, social, and political changes in two South Indian villages.

Isaacs, Harold. *India's Ex-Untouchables*. New York: John Day, 1965. Fascinating series of articles by a journalist-scholar who went to India and interviewed a sample of untouchables. It is rich in anecdote and implicitly compares the situation and dilemmas of the untouchables to those of the blacks in the United States.

Lynch, Owen M. *The Politics of Untouchability: Social Mobility and Social Change in a City of India*. New York: Columbia University Press, 1969. An excellent description of the social mobility of a former untouchable caste of leather workers in Agra, through conversion to Neo-Buddhism.

Papanek, Gustav F. *Pakistan's Development, Social Goals and Private Incentives*. Cambridge: Harvard University Press, 1967. An overly optimistic analysis of Pakistani economic development by a former member of Harvard Advisory Group to the Planning Commission of Pakistan.

Rosen, George. *Democracy and Economic Change in India*. Berkeley:

University of California Press, 1966. A general analysis of India's major problems of political and economic development in the period since independence. The author assesses the gainers and losers from India's Five-Year Plans and suggests alternative paths of action and their implications for United States' policy.

Sayeed, K.B. *The Political System of Pakistan.* Boston: Houghton Mifflin, 1967. Deals with problems of economic development as well as with politics and foreign policy. The author also relates Pakistan's regional stresses to economic, political, and social developments.

Turner, Roy (ed.). *India's Urban Future.* Bombay: Oxford University Press, 1962. A valuable collection of articles on India's urban problems and on some of the theoretical and practical difficulties faced by scholars and administrators in this field.

Discussion Topics and Questions

1. Discuss the problems in raising agricultural output in India and Pakistan.
2. How has industry fared in the private and public sectors in India since independence?
3. Discuss the position of untouchables in India.
4. Compare student political activity in India, Pakistan, and Western countries.
5. What effects has economic planning had on Indian and Pakistani villages?

XX. PROBLEMS OF INDEPENDENCE FOR INDIA AND PAKISTAN: INTERNAL POLITICS

A. India
  1. Present period of flux
    a. One-party dominance, 1947–1967, seriously undermined
    b. Splintering of parties, creation and failure of alliances continue apace
    c. Serious challenges to stability from right, left, regional forces
  2. Government of India
    a. Secular state provided for in Congress traditions, constitution
    b. Parliamentary system with two-house legislature at center

c. President indirectly elected with variable powers
   d. Federal system with fairly strong state governments, but center has powers to rule states in some circumstances
   e. Organization of states along linguistic lines (see XIX)
   f. Constitution, 1950, provides for Fundamental Rights; can be limited during emergency periods
   g. Supreme Court at center and state high courts
   h. Civil servants in Indian Administrative Service man bureaucracy
3. Congress rule: legacy of nationalist period
   a. Provides Prime Ministers, cabinets at center, 1947 to present
      1) Jawaharlal Nehru, 1947–1964; Lal Bahadur Shastri, 1964–1966; Indira Gandhi, 1966 to present
      2) Dominance at center threatened by split in party; Mrs. Gandhi's Congress (Reformed) wins two-thirds in 1971 election for Lok Sabha
   b. In the states
      1) Holds control in almost all states, 1947–1967
      2) Loses majority in more than half states, 1967 election
      3) Diverse patterns of alliances and presidential rule in some states since 1967
   c. Congress support
      1) Before independence among wealthy on land and in business; some peasants, intellectuals, students, professionals
      2) Rise of other parties since 1947 cuts Congress support, while universal franchise helps to broaden it
      3) Support of rich peasants, business, professionals continues
4. Indian communist parties
   a. Split into three major groups, some minor ones
   b. Division between official C.P.I. (Communist Party of India) and C.P.I. (Marxist), early 1960s
      1) Official C.P.I. aligned with Soviets; fading electoral strength
      2) C.P.I. (M) more peasant, Chinese orientation; gaining electoral strength
   c. Rise of Naxalities after 1967; attempts to organize C.P.I. (Marxist-Leninist)
      1) Advocate violent uprising in countryside

162

2) Denounce other C.P.I.'s as false communists for their electoral participation, working in system

d. Communists strong West Bengal, Andhra, Kerala

e. Weak in other areas, so cannot present real national alternative

5. Parties on the right

a. Swatantra Party, founded 1959

1) Business and rural wealthy support it

2) Tied to princes, landlords in Rajasthan, Bihar, Orissa

3) Leaders include old, dissident Congressmen, Socialists

4) Win 44 seats in Lok Sabha in 1967; largest opposition party

b. Jana Sangh

1) Eclectic mixture of tradition and modernity

2) Emphasize Hindu culture, Hindi as national language

3) Strongly against secular state idea and Pakistan

4) Strength in Hindi-speaking areas, among lower middle class

5) Ties to R.S.S. (Rashtriya Swayamsevak Sangh), paramilitary Hindu organization founded in 1925

6. Regional, communal, caste forces in Indian politics

a. Regional parties strong in some areas

1) D.M.K. (Dravida Munnetra Kazhagam) in Madras

a) Heir of Justice Party wins majority in Madras and 25 seats in Lok Sabha, 1967 election

b) Aims to protect Tamil culture, southern interests against Hindi encroachments

2) Akali Dal in Punjab, both regional and communal

a) Backing among Sikh community

b) Wins fight for Punjabi Suba, separate state with Sikh majority, 1966

b. Caste factors taken into account by all parties

1) Candidates often chosen from majority or large caste group

2) Caste associations give castes leverage in political work

c. Communal factors: Hindus, Muslims, Sikhs use communal organization, appeals

7. Functions, roles, idioms of Indian politicians

a. Politicians dispense scarce resources; enforcement capabilities

b. Help link rural areas into state and national politics

163

c. Use modern, traditional appeals, idioms

d. Saintly or apolitical involvement in public affairs by Vinoba Bhave, Jayaprakash Narayan

B. Pakistan

  1. Legacies of Pakistan movement

    a. Islamic fervor, but weak party organization and lack of concrete program

    b. Charismatic figure, Jinnah, dies 1948

    c. Lack of administrators and poor financial condition

    d. Opportunities in independent nation that were not available under British Raj or in Hindu-majority state

  2. Period of parliamentary rule, 1947–1958

    a. Frequent breakdowns of parliamentary system

    b. Lack of any national party

    c. Tensions between civil servants, army, and politicians

  3. Ayub period, 1958–1968

    a. Rise of Ayub

      1) Army head from 1951

      2) Moves in when politicians falter

    b. Martial law, 1958–1962

      1) Crackdown on politicians

      2) In British Raj's viceregal tradition

    c. Constitutional autocracy, 1962–1969

      1) System of Basic Democracy set up under 1962 constitution

        a) Limited election system with 80,000 Basic Democrats

        b) Based mostly on rich farmers, feudal factions which support status quo

      2) National Assembly has limited functions, powers

      3) President Ayub controls budget, provinces

      4) Opposition lawyers, courts function as slight check on regime

      5) Ayub's backing among landlords, army, entrepreneurs

  4. Fall of Ayub

    a. Pressure of political groups, students leads to resignation, 1968

    b. In failing health

    c. Military rule continues under General (now President) Yahya Khan

    d. Promise of elections late 1970

  5. Regional strains

    a. Greatest strain between East and West Pakistan

164

1) Many in East feel exploited by West and central government
2) East earns much of foreign exchange, gets smaller cut of development funds, investment
3) Cultural issue: strength of Bengali and Bengali identity in East; language riots, 1952
4) East antipathy evident in crushing defeat of Muslim League in 1954 election at hands of Fazlul Huq-H.S. Suhrawardy coalition
5) Riots between Bengali and non-Bengali Muslims
6) Center's continued interference in East's politics
7) Continued demands for more East autonomy
8) Sheik Mujibur Rahman's Awami League Party wins majority of seats in Constituent Assembly, 1971
9) Political negotiations between President Yahya Khan and leaders from East and West Pakistan fail in March 1971
10) President moves militarily to crush Awami League and movement for independent Bangla Desh from late March 1971
11) Widespread resistance by irregular forces in East against Pakistani army and declaration of independent nation of Bangla Desh
   b. Regional feelings also in West, mainly against Punjabi dominance
6. Religion and politics
   a. Question of role of Islam in political life debated: how democracy, socialism, property rights to be defined in Islamic state
   b. 1962 Constitution: Advisory Council of Islamic Ideology
   c. Islam used by politicians
      1) More secular, modern types refer to it: Ayub, Chaudhri Mohammad Ali
      2) Fundamentalist movement of Maulana Maudoodi: Jamaat-i-Islami
      3) Pirs, ulamas political influence in rural areas

Reading Assignments

Brecher, *Nehru,* chapters XV, XVI, XVII, XX
Brown, *United States and India and Pakistan,* chapters 11, 12
Sources of Indian Tradition, 831–76, 878–87, 924–31; paperback, 279–324, 326–35, 372–79

Optional Assignments

Bailey, F.G. *Politics and Social Change. Orissa in 1959.* Berkeley: University of California Press, 1963 and paperback. One of the most suggestive and intelligent works on Indian society and politics. The author is an anthropologist who analyzes politics at the village, constituency, and state levels. He asks what politics means to participants at these levels and how the levels are linked together.

Sayeed, K.B. *The Politics of Pakistan.* See XIX.

Additional Readings

Binder, Leonard. *Religion and Politics in Pakistan.* Berkeley: University of California Press, 1961. A valuable study of the role religious groups played in the formulation of the constitution of Pakistan, and of the political dilemmas of an Islamic nation confronting modern problems.

Harrison, Selig S. *India: The Most Dangerous Decades.* Princeton: Princeton University Press, 1960. Controversial and stimulating analysis of the centrifugal forces at work in India. The author devotes several chapters to the aims and methods of Indian Communists, particularly in South India.

Morris-Jones, W.H. *The Government and Politics of India.* London: Hutchinson, 1964. A good, general account of Indian politics. The author develops his idea of three idioms of politics used in India: the traditional, the modern, and the saintly.

Overstreet, Gene D., and Marshall Windmiller. *Communism in India.* See XIV.

Rudolph, Lloyd I., and Susanne Hoeber Rudolph. *The Modernity of Tradition.* Chicago: University of Chicago Press, 1967. A suggestive collection of essays focusing on caste and politics, on Gandhi's development and place in Indian society, and on legal cultures in India.

Weiner, Myron. *Party Politics in India.* Princeton: Princeton University Press, 1957. Invaluable study of party cleavages and alliances, dealing mainly with developments in the decade following independence. The author explores both right- and left-wing politics.

Weiner, Myron. *Party Building in a New Nation.* Chicago: University of Chicago Press, 1967. A first-rate study of the Congress party concentrating on five districts of India to give depth and detail to the analysis. The author conducted extensive interviews with political workers in the five districts during 1961 to 1963.

Weiner, Myron (ed.). *State Politics in India.* Princeton: Princeton University Press, 1968. Uneven but important essays on the politics of the different Indian states by scholars from the United States, Canada, Britain, and India

Discussion Topics and Questions

1. Discuss the working of the parliamentary system in India. Analyze the forces working for and against its continuation.
2. Discuss the failure of party politics in Pakistan.
3. Analyze the social and economic bases of the different political parties in India. Do parties have different economic bases in different regions?
4. Discuss the meaning of state and national politics for an Indian villager.
5. Discuss the possibilities for a movement to the left or to the right in Indian politics.
6. How justified are the claims of East Pakistanis that they are exploited by West Pakistani leaders?

Maps

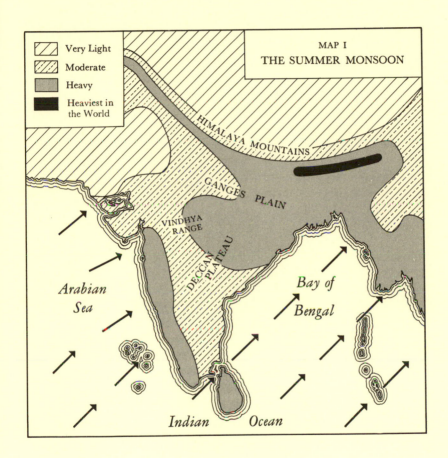

Very Light
Moderate
Heavy
Heaviest in the World

MAP I
THE SUMMER MONSOON

HIMALAYA MOUNTAINS

GANGES PLAIN

VINDHYA RANGE

DECCAN PLATEAU

Arabian Sea

Bay of Bengal

Indian Ocean

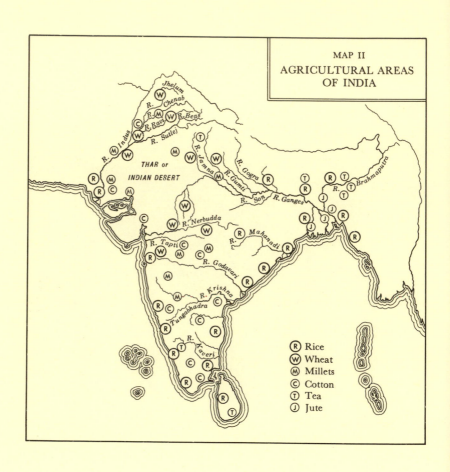

MAP II
AGRICULTURAL AREAS
OF INDIA

Ⓡ Rice
Ⓦ Wheat
Ⓜ Millets
Ⓒ Cotton
Ⓣ Tea
Ⓙ Jute

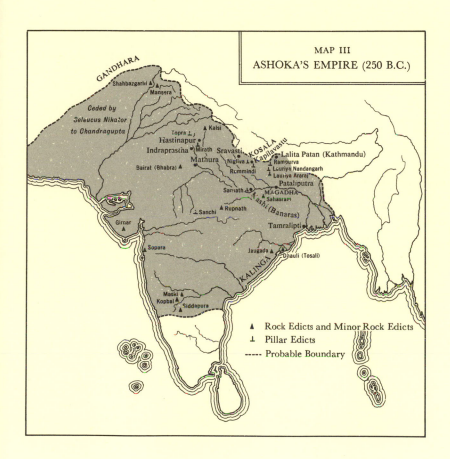

MAP III

ASHOKA'S EMPIRE (250 B.C.)

GANDHARA

Shahbazgarhi

Mansera

Ceded by
Seleucus Nikator
to Chandragupta

Topra
Kalsi

Hastinapur

Indraprastha
Mirath
Sravasti
KOSALA
Kapilavastu
Lalita Patan (Kathmandu)

Mathura
Nigliva
Rampurva

Bairat (Bhabra)
Rummindi
Lauriya Nandangarh
Lauriya Araraj

Pataliputra

Sarnath
MAGADHA
Kashi (Banaras)
Sahasram

Girnar
Sanchi
Rupnath

Tamralipti

Sopara

Jaugada
Dhauli (Tosali)

KALINGA

Maski
Kopbal
Siddapura

▲ Rock Edicts and Minor Rock Edicts

⊥ Pillar Edicts

----- Probable Boundary

171

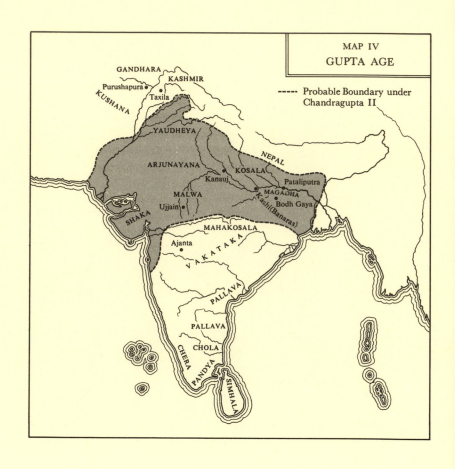

MAP IV

GUPTA AGE

----- Probable Boundary under
Chandragupta II

GANDHARA

KASHMIR

Purushapura

KUSHANA

Taxila

YAUDHEYA

NEPAL

ARJUNAYANA

KOSALA

Kanauj

Pataliputra

MALWA

MAGADHA

Kashi(Banaras)

Bodh Gaya

Ujjain

SHAKA

MAHAKOSALA

Ajanta

VAKATAKA

PALLAVA

PALLAVA

CHERA

CHOLA

PANDYA

SIMHALA

172

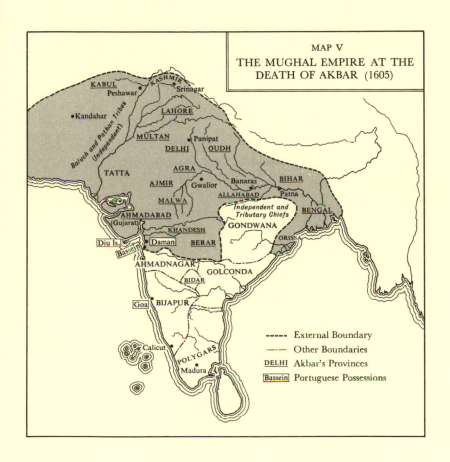

MAP V

THE MUGHAL EMPIRE AT THE
DEATH OF AKBAR (1605)

KABUL
Peshawar
KASHMIR
Srinagar
Kandahar
Baluch and Pathan Tribes
(Independent)
LAHORE
MULTAN
Panipat
DELHI
OUDH
TATTA
AGRA
AJMIR
Gwalior
Banaras
BIHAR
MALWA
ALLAHABAD
Patna
BENGAL
Independent and
Tributary Chiefs
GONDWANA
AHMADABAD
(Gujarat)
KHANDESH
Diu Is.
Bassein
Daman
BERAR
ORISSA
AHMADNAGAR
GOLCONDA
BIDAR
Goa
BIJAPUR
Calicut
POLYGARS
Madura

- - - - - External Boundary
— · — Other Boundaries
DELHI Akbar's Provinces
Bassein Portuguese Possessions

173

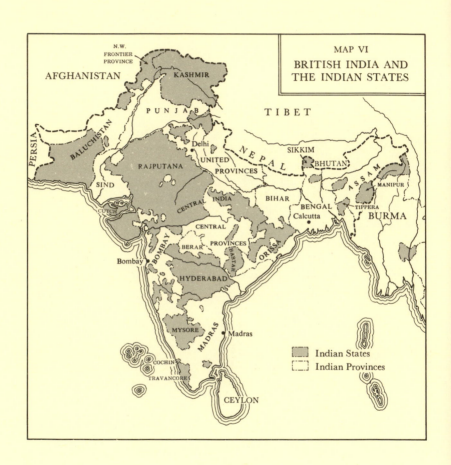

MAP VI
BRITISH INDIA AND
THE INDIAN STATES

N.W. FRONTIER PROVINCE

AFGHANISTAN

KASHMIR

PUNJAB

TIBET

PERSIA

BALUCHISTAN

SIND

Delhi

UNITED PROVINCES

NEPAL

SIKKIM

BHUTAN

ASSAM

MANIPUR

RAJPUTANA

CENTRAL INDIA

BIHAR

BENGAL

Calcutta

TIPPERA

BURMA

CUTCH

CENTRAL PROVINCES

BERAR

BASTAR

ORISSA

BOMBAY

Bombay

HYDERABAD

MYSORE

MADRAS

Madras

COCHIN

TRAVANCORE

CEYLON

Indian States
Indian Provinces

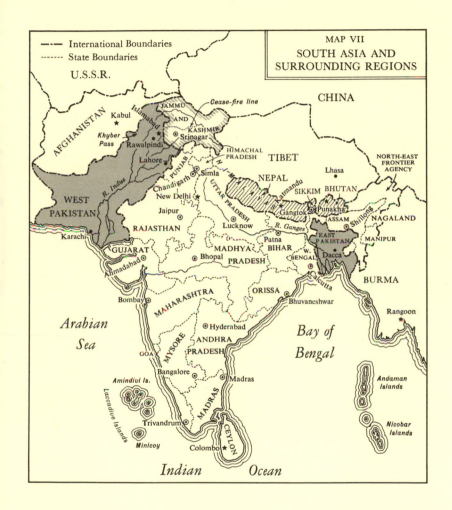

U.S.S.R.

CHINA

AFGHANISTAN

Kabul ★

Islamabad

Cease-fire line

JAMMU
AND
KASHMIR

*Khyber
Pass*

Rawalpindi ★

Srinagar ⊙

HIMACHAL
PRADESH

TIBET

NORTH-EAST
FRONTIER
AGENCY

Lahore ⊙

R. Indus

PUNJAB

Simla ⊙

H. J. MTS.

NEPAL

Lhasa ⊙

Chandigarh ⊙

New Delhi ★

UTTAR PRADESH

Katmandu

SIKKIM

BHUTAN

Gangtok ⊙

Punakha ★

SHILLONG

NAGALAND

WEST
PAKISTAN

Jaipur ⊙

ASSAM

Karachi ⊙

RAJASTHAN

Lucknow ⊙

R. Ganges

EAST
PAKISTAN

MANIPUR

GUJARAT

MADHYA
PRADESH

Patna ⊙

BIHAR

W. L.
BENGAL

Dacca ⊙

Ahmadabad ⊙

Bhopal ⊙

Calcutta

BURMA

*Arabian
Sea*

Bombay ⊙

MAHARASHTRA

ORISSA

Bhuvaneshwar ⊙

Rangoon ★

*Bay of
Bengal*

Hyderabad ⊙

ANDHRA
PRADESH

*Andaman
Islands*

GOA

MYSORE

Amindivi Is.

Bangalore ⊙

Madras ⊙

Laccadive Islands

MADRAS

*Nicobar
Islands*

Trivandrum ⊙

CEYLON

Minicoy

Colombo ★

Indian   Ocean

PRONUNCIATION GUIDE

The majority of Indic vocabulary used in the syllabus is drawn from Sanskrit, Arabic, Persian, and Hindi. Indic terms and proper names are anglicized in accordance with the spelling in *Webster's Third New International Dictionary*, except that Sanskrit *ś* (palatal sibilant) is rendered as *sh;* e.g. Sanskrit Śiva is anglicized Shiva. Transliterated forms of anglicized terms appear in italics in the glossary. Titles of specific literary works also appear in transliteration. The system of romanization and diacritical marks used is the system of transliteration found in Louis Renou's *Grammaire Sanskrite* (Paris, 1930), pp. xi–xiii, with the exception that here *ś* is used for *ç*.

Vowels are given their full value, as in Italian or German:

a   as *u* in c*u*t
ā   as *a* in f*a*ther
i   as *i* in p*i*t
ī   as *i* in mach*i*ne
u   as *u* in p*u*t
ū   as *u* in r*u*le
ṛ   a short vowel; as *ri* in *ri*ver
e   as *ay* in s*ay*
ai   as *ai* in *ai*sle
o   as *o* in g*o*
au   as *ow* in c*ow*
ṁ   nasalizes and lengthens the preceding vowel
ḥ   a rough breathing, replacing an original *s* or *r;* lengthens the preceding vowel and occurs only at the end of a syllable or word

176

It should be noted that the aspirated consonants *kh, gh, ch, jh,*
th, dh, ph, bh, and so on are considered single consonants in the
Sanskrit alphabet. Most consonants are analogous to the English,
if the distinction between aspirated and nonaspirated consonants is
observed; for example, the aspirated consonants *th* and *ph* must
never be pronounced as in English *th*in and *ph*ial, but as in
ho*th*ouse and she*ph*erd. (Similarly, *kh, gh, ch, jh, dh, bh.*) The differences between the Sanskrit "cerebral" *ṭ, ṭh, ḍ, ḍh, ṇ,* and "den-
tal" *t, th, d, dh, n* are another distinctive feature of the language.

Note also:

g	as *g* in *g*oat
ṅ	as *n* in i*n*k, or si*ng*
c	as *ch* in *ch*urch
ñ	as *ñ* in se*ñ*or (Spanish)
ś, ṣ	as *sh* in *sh*ape or *s* in *s*ugar; both anglicized as *sh*

GLOSSARY OF BASIC INDIC
TERMS

AHIMSA (Skt. *ahiṁsā,* "non-injury")   The Jain and Buddhist doctrine of refraining from taking life; later incorporated into Vaishnava and Gandhian thought.

ARTHA (Skt.)   Worldly success, wealth; regarded by Hindus as one of a man's four legitimate pursuits in life. Kautilya's *Arthaśāstra* deals with polity and administration.

ARYAN (Skt. *ārya*)   The term by which the Indo-European-speaking invaders of India designated themselves; thus they are known as "Aryans," ("noble," "respectable"), denoting their racial and moral superiority, as opposed to the pre-existing peoples of India (called *an-ārya*). Buddhism: aryasatya (Pali *ariyasacca*) Four "noble truths," nucleus of Buddha's first sermon.

ATMAN (Skt. *ātman*)   Life breath, microcosmic life principle equated with the universal absolute (brahman) in Vedanta.

BHAKTI (Skt. "devotion")   Religious devotion, directed towards a personal deity. Devotion is a discipline (bhaktiyoga) in the *Bhagavad Gītā;* stress on love in medieval bhakti movements.

BHOODAN (Skt. *bhūdān,* "land-gift")   Vinobha Bhave's movement for land reform through voluntary donations from landowners to landless peasants. Example of the use of religion in politics.

BODHISATTVA (Skt. "one whose essence is enlightenment")   In Theravada Buddhism, a previous incarnation of Buddha. In Mahayana, a being who compassionately refrains from entering Nirvana to save others and is worshipped as a deity.

BRAHMAN (Skt.)   [1] Prayer, the sacred word and its magical force; in Vedanta the ultimate absolute underlying the universe. [2] Priest, one who prays (capitalized for distinction; also

178

Brahmin); the first of the four classes or ranks of Hindu society. Adj. Brahmanic, pertaining to members of this class and their doctrines.

BUDDHA (Skt. "enlightened") A person who has attained enlightenment; particularly Siddhartha Gautama, who founded Buddhism in the sixth century B.C.

CHARKHA (Hindi *carkhā;* Persian *charkhā;* Skt. *cakra*) Domestic spinning wheel, used mainly for cotton (cf. Khadi); made into a symbol of Indian revival by Gandhi. The wheel itself is a symbol in Buddhism; forms the center of the Indian national flag.

DARSHANA (Skt. *darśana,* "view") Philosophy, as the means for destroying ignorance and achieving freedom; each of the six orthodox Hindu philosophic systems. Also, the vision of a religious image or person.

DHARMA (Skt. "that which is established or firm") Structure of reality. Social custom, sanctified as religious law and duty, relative to one's station in society and life (varnashrama-dharma); codified in the Hindu law books (dharma-shastras). Religion, one of legitimate pursuits in life; Hinduism is called the "eternal religion" (sanatana-dharma). Buddha's doctrine (Pali *dhamma*). Ashoka's concept of universal moral law.

GURU (Skt.) Hindu teacher or spiritual preceptor. Important in Sikh religion as mediator between man and God, applied as a title to the founder and nine leaders of Sikhism.

ISLAM (Ar. *Islām*) "Submission" (to the will of God); the religion founded in the seventh century A.D. by Muhammad, established in India during the medieval period by foreign invaders.

JAJMAN (Hindi *jajmān,* from Skt. *yajamāna,* "patron") A person receiving service from members of various occupational groups as his exclusive and hereditary right. The Jajmani system, prevalent in Northern India, stresses the interdependence of castes in the patron-client relationships.

JATI (Skt. *jāti,* "birth") The common term for caste, the system of social stratification of groups characterized by endogamy, hereditary occupation and status. Cf. Varna.

JINA (Skt. "conqueror") One who has conquered temporal and material existence through self-discipline; particularly Mahavira, who founded Jainism in the sixth century B.C.

KAMA (Skt. *kāma,* "desire") Pleasure, love, longing. Cultivation of erotic and aesthetic pleasure is recognized by Hindus as one of a man's four legitimate pursuits in life. Evils of desire are stressed by religious teachers, e.g. Buddha.

KARMA (Skt. *karman,* "action") Work, performance of one's business. The law of retribution based on volitional action: actions have inevitable moral consequences in this life or the next, determine one's condition; actions generate motive power for the round of rebirths and deaths which bind a man to phenomenal existence. Cf. Samsara.

KHADI (Hindi *khādī* or *khaddar*) Hand-spun, hand-woven cloth associated with the Congress movement against foreign goods. Cf. Swadeshi.

MAYA (Skt. *māyā* "magic," "illusion") The illusion-creating power of a god or demon; the energy that creates the cosmic illusion that the phenomenal world is real (especially in Vedanta).

MOKSHA (Skt. *mokṣa,* "release") Liberation from the bondage of finite existence; regarded by Hindus as one of a man's four legitimate pursuits in life, attainable by extra-mundane means.

NAWAB, also NABOB (Hindi *nawāb*) A governor of a Mughal province; under the British, a Muslim ruler of a princely state. Cf. Raja. Also a term used for those Europeans believed to have made great fortunes in the eighteenth century.

NIRVANA (Skt. *nirvāṇa* "blowing out," "extinction") Buddhist term for the goal of life, i.e., the cessation of phenomenal existence and freedom from karma (cf. Samsara).

PANCHAYAT (Hindi *pañcāyat*) An elective council of about five members (Skt. *pañca =* five) organized in independent India as an organ of village self-government; based on a traditional group of five members acknowledged as the governing body of a village or caste; also the process of resolving disputes.

RASA (Skt. "flavor," "emotion") Aesthetic emotion; the emotional atmosphere which a poem or play creates is the essence of Indian aesthetic experience; related to religious bliss (especially in bhakti literature).

RAJA (Skt. *rājā*) Chief, king; maharaja = "great king," a title claimed by Hindu rulers of princely states. Cf. Nawab.

RYOTWARI (Hindi *raiyat,* "peasant") A system of collecting land rent or taxes in which government settlement was made directly with ryot, usually a manager of actual tillers of the soil; in South India often high caste; also middle or upper peasants who may have considerable holdings. Cf. Zamindar, who is a manager of managers, one level further removed from actual tillers.

SAHIB (Hindi [from Ar.] *sāhib,* "master") Applied as an honorific to Europeans in India.

SAMSARA (Skt. *saṁsāra*) Transmigration: the indefinitely re-
peated cycles of birth, misery, and death caused by karma; phenomenal existence (cf. Nirvana).

SATYAGRAHA (Skt. *satyāgraha,* "truth-force" or "firm adherence
to truth") The term coined by Gandhi for his method of nonviolent resistance.

SEPOY (Hindi *sipāhī,* "soldier") Refers particularly to an Indian
soldier in the employ of the British.

SIKH (Hindi "disciple," from Skt. *śiṣya*) A follower of Guru
Nanak, founder of the militant Punjabi community, later defiant
of Muslim rule.

SUFI (Pers. *sūfī*) Refers to groups of Muslim mystics who believed
in the possibility of immediate knowledge and union with the
divine; influential in converting Hindus to Islam during medieval period.

SWADESHI (Skt. *sva-deśin* "of one's own country," "native") The
boycott of foreign goods, especially cloth, associated with the
independence movement. Cf. Khadi, Swaraj.

SWARAJ (Skt. *svarājya,* "self-rule") Home rule or independence.
The goal of the nationalist movement.

VARNA (Skt. "class") Refers to the theoretical division of Hindu
society into four classes or ranks (cf. Jati). Varnashrama-dharma
is the notion that religious law and duty are relative to a man's
position in society and stage of life.

VEDANTA (Skt. *vedānta,* "the end of the Veda") Refers to the
Upanishads and the influential school of Hindu philosophy based
on the Upanishads.

ZAMINDAR (Hindi *zamīndār,* "holder of land") Refers mainly
to Hindu landholders, revenue collectors under Mughal and
British rule.

YOGA (Skt. "yoking," "union," "discipline") Psychophysical
method of "discipline" for achieving liberation; one of the six
systems of orthodox Hindu philosophy. "Union" of the self with
the Universal Spirit. Various disciplines in the *Bhagavad Gītā,*
e.g. karmayoga, bhaktiyoga.

GUIDE TO ILLUSTRATIVE
MATERIALS

The best source for current information of audiovisual materials on India is The Educational Resources Center, The University of the State of New York, 11 West 42nd Street, New York, New York 10036.

Another good source for general information on illustrative materials is The Asia Society, 112 East 64th Street, New York, New York 10021. *A Guide to Films, Filmstrips, Maps and Globes, Records on Asia* and the *Supplement* to this guide are useful brochures published by The Asia Society.

The *Newsletter* of the Association for Asian Studies, published quarterly, contains a valuable section on "Instructional Programs and Teaching Materials," giving current information on special programs and new illustrative materials. The *Newsletter* is sent to members of the Association. A subscription for nonmembers is $2.50 per year, available through the Association for Asian Studies, Inc., P.O. Box 606, Ann Arbor, Michigan 48104.

A limited number of interesting films produced by the Films Division of the Government of India are available on free loan from the Indian Embassy and Consulates. *Motion Pictures for the Study of India: A Guide to Classroom Films* by Theodore M. Vestal, a pamphlet published by The Educational Resources Center, describes about twenty good films and lists sources for rental and/or purchase.